# The Oxford Book of Contemporary New Zealand Poetry

chosen by
Fleur Adcock

Auckland
Oxford University Press

*Oxford University Press*

Oxford   London   Glasgow
New York   Toronto   Melbourne   Auckland
Kuala Lumpur   Singapore   Hong Kong   Tokyo
Delhi   Bombay   Calcutta   Madras   Karachi
Nairobi   Dar Es Salaam   Cape Town
and associates in
Beirut   Berlin   Ibadan   Mexico City   Nicosia

First published 1982
Introduction and selection © Fleur Adcock 1982

ISBN 0 19 558092 3

Cover design by John McNulty

Photoset in Bembo and printed by Whitcoulls Limited, Christchurch
Published by Oxford University Press,
28 Wakefield Street, Auckland, New Zealand

# Contents

# ACKNOWLEDGEMENTS

The editor and publishers gratefully acknowledge permission to reproduce the following copyright material:

Charles Brasch: 'Night Cries, Wakari Hospital' from *Home Ground*, Caxton Press, 1974. Allen Curnow: '8: The Kitchen Cupboard' and '10: A Framed Photograph' from *Trees, Effigies, Moving Objects*, Catspaw Press, 1972; 'This Beach can be Dangerous' from *An Abominable Temper*, Catspaw Press, 1973; 'Canst Thou Draw Out Leviathan with an Hook?', 'A Balanced Bait in Handy Pellet Form', 'Dichtung und Wahrheit', 'Bring Your Own Victim', 'An Incorrigible Music' from *An Incorrigible Music*, AUP/OUP, 1979; 'A Reliable Service', 'An Excellent Memory', 'You Will Know When You Get There' from *London Magazine*.
Kendrick Smithyman: 'An Ordinary Day Beyond Kaitaia' from *Earthquake Weather*, AUP/OUP, 1972; 'Friday Night' and 'Resort' from *Dwarf with a Billiard Cue*, AUP/OUP, 1978; 'The Last Moriori' from *Islands*.
Hone Tuwhare: 'Ron Mason' from *Selected Poems*, John McIndoe, 1980; 'A Burnt Offering to your Greenstone Eyes, Tangaroa' from *Comment*; 'Snowfall' from *NZ Listener*.
Louis Johnson: 'How to Measure a Cat' from *Islands*; 'Coming and Going' from *Landfall*; 'This Particular Christian' from *Salient*.
Lauris Edmond: 'Commercial Traveller' from *In Middle Air*, Pegasus, 1975; '3 a.m.' from *The Pear Tree*, Pegasus, 1977; 'Section XI' *Wellington Letter*, Mallinson Rendel, 1980; 'Three Women', 'Town Ghost', 'A Difficult Adjustment', 'Love Poem', 'The Names' from *Salt from the North*, OUP, 1980; 'Going to Moscow'.
Alistair Campbell: 'The Dark Lord of Savaiki' from *Collected Poems*, Alister Taylor, 1982.
James K. Baxter: Jerusalem Sonnets 1, 18, 35, 36, 37, 'The Ikons', 'He Waiata mo Te Kare', Autumn Testament sonnets 15, 19, 22, 29, 32, 42, 46, section 3 of 'How to Fly by Standing Still' all from *Collected Poems*, OUP, 1979.
C. K. Stead: Twenty-one Sonnets, 1, 2, 6, 9; 'The Young Wife'; 'Art has nothing to do . . .' and 'October she phoned . . .' all from *Walking Westward*, The Shed, 1979; 'This may be your captain speaking' from *NZ Listener*.
Vincent O'Sullivan: 'Talking to Her' from *Bearings*, OUP, 1973; 'Bus Stop' from *From the Indian Funeral*, John McIndoe, 1976; Sections 8, 9, 13, 15, 31, 32, 33, 35, 44 from *Brother Jonathan, Brother Kafka*, OUP, 1980; 'Late Lunch, San Antonio' and 'Further Instructions'.
Michael Jackson: 'Sudan', 'The Red Flag' from *Latitudes of Exile*, John McIndoe, 1976; 'Australia', 'Neanderthal', 'Mask-maker', from *Wall*, John McIndoe, 1980.
Alan Loney: 'Of flowers' from *Shorter Poems 1963-1977*, AUP/OUP, 1979; 'Elegy 1', 'The eternal return', 'Elegy 2', 'Elegy 6' from *dear Mondrian*, Hawk Press, 1976.
Rachel McAlpine: 'the test' from *Islands*; 'three poems for your eyes' from *Stay at the Dinner Party*, Caveman, 1977; 'on the train' from *Fancy Dress*, Cicada, 1979.
David Mitchell: 'windfall', 'celebrant' from *Pipe Dreams in Ponsonby*, Caveman, 1975.
Elizabeth Smither: 'Song about my father' from *Here come the clouds*, Alister Taylor, 1975; 'Sugar Daddy', 'The beak', 'The Feast of All Saints' from *You're very seductive William Carlos Williams*, John McIndoe, 1978; 'Change of school' from *Landfall*; 'Fr Anselm

fitting Williams and Br Leander Neville . . ' from *The Legend of Marcello Mastroianni's Wife*, AUP/OUP, 1981.

Sam Hunt: 'Notes from a Journey', 'Stabat Mater', 'April Fool' from *Collected Poems*, Penguin, 1980.

Bill Manhire: 'The elaboration' from *The Elaboration*, Square & Circle, 1972; 'The poetry reading', 'The collection', 'Summer', 'The importance of personal relationships' from *How to Take Off Your Clothes at the Picnic*, Wai-Te-Ata Press, 1977; 'Wulf', 'Wellington', 'Party Going', 'Last things', from *Good Looks*, AUP/OUP, 1982.

Ian Wedde: 'Losing the Straight Way' from *Spells for Coming Out*, AUP/OUP, 1977; Sonnets 2, 9, 10, 53 from *Earthly: Sonnets for Carlos*, Amphedesma Press, 1975; 'Cardrona Valley', 'Beautiful Poultry', 'Dark Wood', from *Castaly*, AUP/OUP, 1980; 'Hardon ('get one today'' from *Islands*.

Tony Beyer: 'Cornwallis', 'The Seventies', 'A Comfort Stop', 'Cut Lilac' from *Dancing Bear*, Melaleuca Press, 1981.

Murray Edmond: 'An Afternoon in the Garden' from *Patchwork*, Hawk Press, 1978; 'Telephoning It', 'Stopping the Heart', 'My Return to Czechoslovakia' from *End Wall*, OUP, 1981.

Cilla McQueen: 'Matinal' from *Islands*; 'Weekend Sonnets'; 'To Ben, at the lake' from *NZ Listener*.

# INTRODUCTION

This is an anthology of native New Zealand poetry: the word 'indigenous' needs to be understood as silently present in the title. It is the home-grown product that I have set out to exhibit, not the work of visitors to this country or expatriates abroad. Poems by immigrant Englishmen and Americans may have added variety to the pages of local magazines, but they did not arise out of the particular circumstances which fostered the writing of New Zealand-bred poets, and it was poetry created in the light of these circumstances, of this social and political climate, that the title of the anthology seemed to me to imply. It could be argued that certain immigrant writers have influenced the work of their contemporaries (as Peter Bland did in the 1960s); but if more recent arrivals from abroad have had such an effect it was only as the mediators of American and European influences which were in any case already operating here. I do not think any significant talent has been excluded from my selection by this criterion.

Expatriates at first posed a trickier problem. It was clear to me that my own work should be excluded, together with that of several others, on the grounds that it has for many years been published abroad and belongs to a different tradition; but I was reluctant to omit the work of Kevin Ireland, who in spite of twenty years' residence in London has kept in close touch with New Zealand and has consistently published here. In the end, though, questions of space settled the matter: with such a limited number of pages at my disposal I thought it best to devote them all to poets actually living here. Naturally a year or two spent overseas was no disqualification – rather the opposite: it is usually good for the imagination – but the decision to settle permanently in another country leads to a subtle but distinct alteration in one's consciousness and attitudes; without ceasing to be a New Zealander one develops a view of the world whose focus is elsewhere, and it seems to me that poetry written from such an outlook cannot rightly be called New Zealand poetry.

These somewhat rigid boundaries to my field of selection were dictated not by chauvinism but by tidiness and, I believe, honesty: I saw no harm in making a stance against the over-hospitable behaviour of those anthologists who claim Albert Wendt as a New Zealand writer

...se he happened to be educated here, or those librarians who classify as 'New Zealand literature' books by authors who spent no more than the first few months of their lives in this country. Let's not be greedy. For the purposes of this anthology a New Zealand poet is one who was brought up (not necessarily born) here and has stayed.

As for my definition of the word 'contemporary', most of these poems were first published in the 1970s or later. But books and magazines published after 1970 may well include poems written before that date; sometimes this is clear, but in cases where it is not I have not gone to the lengths of interrogating poets as to when their work was composed. Also I wanted to include a selection from Baxter's *Jerusalem Sonnets*, a significant and influential sequence written in 1969; this therefore stands right at the beginning of the period covered here; most of the other work I have chosen is more recent.

So much for my geographical and temporal guidelines. Looking at the poetry itself, I tried to strike a balance between what was important in the sense that it had claimed wide attention or influenced other writers, and what was interesting, fresh or inventive in itself (with a slight bias towards the latter). Often these categories overlap, but not always. Poetry in New Zealand is an introspective art; its practitioners and readers tend to analyse trends almost before they have occurred and to enter into critical controversy about styles and allegiances. The 1970s were dominated by a discussion of open form and its associated practices, expressed in serious critical articles by C. K. Stead and others and in a good deal of petty argument which still continues. It was natural that a movement away from the British influences which prevailed up to the early 1960s should occur – all Commonwealth countries go through this anti-imperialist phase in their literatures – but its rapturous support by certain critics has come to seem like an attempt to impose a new orthodoxy, an insistence that poetry should now be written in one way only. However, the poets themselves have continued to write in a number of different ways, as I hope my selection will demonstrate.

The first few names in the list of contributors would not surprise anyone who had read no New Zealand poetry since the first edition of Vincent O'Sullivan's *An Anthology of Twentieth Century New Zealand Poetry* appeared in 1970. That Brasch, Curnow and Smithyman would continue writing might have been expected – assuming that they lived, that is. Charles Brasch unfortunately died in 1973; the sequence included here was among the last poetry he wrote, and it seems ⟨...⟩ that this volume should open with so honest, tentative and courageous a leave-taking.

But merely to assume that the established poets would go on writing as before would have been naive. Things are not so simple: poets stop writing (as Curnow apparently did for some years, until his impressive return from silence with *Trees, Effigies, Moving Objects* in 1972), or they decline into repetition and self-parody. And to go on just as before is in any case a pretty meagre achievement. In choosing work by the older poets I have looked for at least a strengthening of existing skills if not the development of new ones. Brasch was among those who did not stand still but remained open to experience and curious about ways of representing it.

Other names from his generation may be missed here. Denis Glover, who died in 1980, never took himself seriously as a poet, and in his later years concentrated largely upon being an entertaining old buffer. The verse-doodlings of this period can hardly be placed beside his former achievement: the love poems are touching but don't quite come off, and the rest tends to be slight. In 'Mick Stimpson' he returned to one of the solitary characters who had figured in his earlier work and wrote with something of his old touch, but the poem is too long to include in full and token snippets do not stand well alone.

One side-effect of the small society in which New Zealanders live is that large personalities such as Glover and Baxter become well known to us as people, not just as poets, and our affection for them may lend a charm even to their minor and undistinguished efforts: we hear the voice behind the lines, instead of noticing the careless versification. Fortunately for our critical standards this effect is less pronounced when poets are still alive.

James K. Baxter, the youngest of the three prominent poets who died during the decade, needs no allowances made for him. His reputation has increased since his death but was already considerable before his posthumous publications consolidated it further. He was a versatile craftsman and astonishingly prolific: his *Collected Poems* could hardly be crammed into one volume, and their range of tone and feeling – lyrical, bawdy, satirical and reverent – is impressive.

In 1969 his disgust with the materialism he saw in society and its effect on the young took him to live as a 'Christian guru' in the isolated settlement of Jerusalem, and this crucial change in his life led also to a new direction in his verse. In the *Jerusalem Sonnets*, a commentary on his experiences there, he adapted the sonnet form into a finely flexible instrument capable of a variety of tones, from chatty low-key narrative, recording the humble, absurd or unsavoury details of daily life, to a soaring religious lyricism. Part of his new asceticism was a demotion of poetry to a minor role among his interests, but however casually he regarded it his talent would not desert him: 'Colin, you can tell my words are crippled now' he wrote in sonnet 37, but they were not. I should have liked to include more of the sonnets, but decided that some of my space should be given to his slightly less familiar work.

Among the living contributors the oldest, Allen Curnow, is the most distinguished of his generation, a poet of rare technical virtuosity and power. His status was secure well before the publication of *An Incorrigible Music* in 1979, but that book and some more recent poems published in the *London Magazine* in 1981 are evidence that his skills and insights continue to develop. He has always been alert to technical experiment but has retained a recognizably individual voice, sharply intelligent, ironic, and tending to pessimism.

Kendrick Smithyman's markedly idiosyncratic style, sometimes criticized as unnecessarily obscure, seems to be the inevitable outcome of a densely complex habit of thought. His jagged rhythms, wide-ranging allusiveness and unpredictable syntax do not make for easy reading at first encounter, but they offer their own satisfactions and can, with familiarity, become addictive.

Louis Johnson, another prolific poet and one whose social realism made a strong impact in the 1950s and 1960s, almost disqualified himself from inclusion here by leaving New Zealand, seemingly for good, in 1968; but he returned in 1980, and I have included a small sample of his recent work.

Alistair Campbell and Hone Tuwhare are also sparingly represented; their reputations were already formed when the period began, and they have not been highly productive since. Both are Polynesian: Tuwhare is a New Zealand Maori, and Campbell was born in the Cook Islands. It may appear that I have gone out of my way to stress this element in my choice from their work, but as it happened there was no need: references to Maori mythology come naturally to Tuwhare, and in Campbell's case the sequence of poems which I have included is his most substantial recent work.

Somewhere around this point in my list of contributors the concept of poetic generations begins to lose its meaning. Lauris Edmond's date of birth and relatively traditional style place her with Johnson and Campbell, but she began writing late and did not publish a collection until 1975; Ian Wedde is more than twenty years younger than Lauris Edmond but is already a thoroughly mature poet and one whose witty intelligence and inventive vigour have made his influence felt by his elders as well as the imitative young.

In any case I am not so much drawing up a chronology as surveying a field. Naturally, though, this involves a certain amount of looking back to see how it came into being. It is satisfying to watch a poet getting steadily better, as have Vincent O'Sullivan and Murray Edmond, the former loosening up his somewhat congested earlier rhythms and diction to achieve a colloquial fluency informed by serious thought, the latter gradually acquiring control over his springy youthful exuberance.

There is a different kind of pleasure in the sight of an utterly original poet stepping into view with a unique quality of vision and expression apparently fully formed right from the start. Bill Manhire is one such, a sure-footed performer who seems never to have needed to go through a stumbling apprenticeship. Elizabeth Smither has to a lesser degree the knack of creating a singular and memorably odd vignette without apparent effort; her touch is less sure, but every now and then she hits off something to be grateful for.

Others rely less on serendipity. C. K. Stead, an excellent critic as well as a writer of poetry and fiction, is too knowing about his craft to leave effects to chance. He has experimented with various styles during his career, including recently the Baxterian sonnets represented here and a post-Poundian modernism so calculatedly imitative as to read like parody. There is no doubt, though, that he has a genuine poetic impulse and can write with force and wit in his less derivative moments.

As a critic Stead has been accused of preaching a prescriptive orthodoxy, although in his now famous 1979 essay 'From Wystan to Carlos: Modern and Modernism in Recent NZ Poetry' he explicitly denied that he was laying down 'prescriptions which poets should follow'. Whether or not he escapes this charge (to which others, such as Alistair Paterson in his anthology *Fifteen Contemporary Poets*, have laid themselves more patently open), the better poets have persisted in their variousness and show little intention of being preached to.

The poems of four people who happen to have been born in the same year, 1940, give some indication of the range: Michael Jackson writes with conventional orthography and syntax in a style whose muted lyricism takes little account of experimental procedures, although his vision is modern enough and his subject-matter international; Rachel McAlpine's minimal punctuation makes her work look more emancipated, but in fact her fresh, personal poetic voice owes relatively little to literary antecedents. By contrast Alan Loney's adroit and subtle use of open form (and of typography, in which as a printer he is expert) should satisfy the most ardent modernist.

David Mitchell is also given to innovative typography; his two poems in this volume are from his only collection so far published (in 1971, with a second edition in 1975). His work is in effect scored on the page for his speaking voice, and much of what he has produced more recently has been created with public performance in mind. An increase in the number and popularity of poetry readings was part of the general upsurge of poetic activity during the late 1960s and 1970s; it has resulted in a predictable crop of forgettable compositions not sufficiently finished or durable to survive in print, but also in some interesting work. Sam Hunt is the most celebrated example of a poet whose personality has captured the popular imagination and who has achieved local fame and been able to earn a living through publishing and performing his verses.

I am sorry not to have included more women poets. The magazines are full of poems by women, but my reading of them has disappointed me: some are very occasional writers, some still immature, and some vitiated by didactic feminism. A few who interested me because they wrote bravely and honestly about subjects which need to be dealt with proved to be as yet too awkward, careless or unfinished in their techniques. (This is true also of some male writers whom I have had reluctantly to omit.) Then there is the seeming compulsion, particularly among the more publicly visible of the younger women poets, to deck their verse out with the names of colours, jewels, fabrics and furs as if they were stocking a boutique—a form of flirtation with their audience paralleled in the work of some popular male poets by an emphasis on fast cars, booze, and aggressive machismo. These are all of course perfectly legitimate subjects, but obsessions, whether with prettiness or its opposite, make for dull reading, and tend to be accompanied by a refusal to engage with deeper issues.

One considerable problem in making this selection was the current fashion for long sequences or book-length poems; some of the most important work published in the last ten years has appeared in this form. In some examples of it, such as Curnow's *An Incorrigible Music*, the sections are self-contained and can be detached as individual poems which stand well enough on their own, although their significance would be heightened if they were seen in context; in other cases I have had to resort to a certain amount of mangling, which I regret but which does not excessively reduce the impact of the truncated parts. There were a few instances, though, where it would have been quite impossible to print anything but the entire poem.

Another problem was the sheer amount of poetry being published, now that it has become a fashionable art and getting it into print is relatively easy. I have had to be ruthlessly selective. Arthur Baysting's 1973 anthology *The Young New Zealand Poets* had nineteen contributors, of whom several more than the six included here are well worth reading, and these were only a fraction of the poets writing in the 1970s; but some have dropped from sight or turned to other media, and in any case there is simply not room to represent everyone who has at some time produced an attractive poem. I needed to be convinced that a poet was consistently capable of interesting work and not just the passive recipient of one or two stray favours from the muse. For this reason also I have given at least two or three pages to each poet's work.

More space would have let me show a wider sampling of newer (not necessarily younger) poets. As it is all my contributors have appeared in magazines and all but one have published collections; they can be said to have established claims to serious consideration. If they seem to me to stand out from among others with similar claims it is because they have brought intelligence, verve, wit and some variety of technical skill to the shaping of their imaginative conceptions.

Wellington, February 1982

# CHARLES BRASCH

## *Night Cries, Wakari Hospital*

Only the flawlessly beautiful
May be admitted to your presence;
To lift veiled eyes to yours
Perhaps to hear your voice
Even to approach and maybe
Kiss the hem of your garment.
Nothing of that for me
I know, I do not ask.
I do not even dream of it.
Enough that day and night from fabled birth to
    dying
I turn and turn
My ear to the wind
That mutters to itself bemused
Over and over without end
Fumbling with your secret name.


Put off, put off.
Hold back nothing.

Little now remains
Of what seemed self
Of self that seemed;
Hardly a thread
From what self once thought itself
To what is now
If any being remains
Except the weak nameless wind–fluttering
    thread.


I betray myself,
I have no blood
But fear.

*Tempora Mutantur*

Beautiful the strong man in his strength,
Happy the self-reliant.
I too rejoiced once
Walking the earth head high.

Farewell the careless days.
Now I enter another rule
Laboriously piecing together
The hard grammar of dependence.

Thread by thread
Unweave, unmake me
Threadbare one
Naked to your nightwinds,
Over your nameless sands
Namelessly strewn.

Mind or body, body-mind,
Self as light   dust or wind,
I-am that will not be defined.

Mote of sand on the beach
That the passing wind turns over
The sea idly washes,
Blessedness.

Fabled city of Agape, if you exist at all,
You are hidden deep in the wounds of life,
        among the wreckage, the blinding pain.

In different words long, long ago,
Before I was old enough to understand
You had spelt it out; and amazingly

My raw untutored heart remembered
And treasured you for those unforgettable
    words
And for your unknown name, Ferenczi.

But only after forty errant years
Does the city rise and stand breathing before
    me;
Not in its walls, not in its rational laws,
But in that intangible inimitable air,
In the tender speech of eyes and hearts,
In loving-kindness of hands
Whose happiness is unwearying service;
The humblest of them in her own way a healer,
A glowing night-light, a day-flower friend,
Carrying unknown your unknown words.

*It is the physician's love heals the patient.*


*The Way Up is the Way Down*

The contraries compel me.
I go both their ways
As they work together
Down through the maze.


Empty. Empty.
Let me listen to you, emptiness.
You do not ring, like a sea shell.
You are the void
From which we come into being,
To which we return.
Empty myself,
Let me listen.

Is it you
Dark-browed Necessity
Stirring the night about me
Stirring?
Ah, let me sink again
Into your deeps
Down – down
Stilled at last
Beyond stirring
Beyond reaching
Not to rise more.


I am bread, Lord,
For your breaking.

Waters
Dispersed over the earth.

Blood
Poured out thin
Draining down
Into the rocks.

I am your elements, Lord,
In their nothingness.


*Watch-dog*

Gnawing, gnawing the edge of night,
Black-barking dog,
You rend the seamless dark to tatters
The tent of sleep
That held me an oblivious hour.
Faithful guardian, would you destroy me?

*A Word to Peter Olds*

Sleepless through long nights, I think of you
Hived in another cell of this same
House of pain and healing
And hope that you at least sleep darkly
Sealed fast from cries, lights, mechanized
    clamour.

Fellow, fellow-stranger, how can I reach you
By word or sign? We scarcely know each other.
We exchange a smile and greeting in the street
By chance, or in a packed interval at the Globe,
But too much seeming seems to separate us,

Years, custom, the habit of reserve.
Yet I think of you as one who goes
Up the mountain in shadow, where I would go,
Not knowing who I am, or why I must,
With yellow robe and begging bowl.

*Winter Anemones*

The ruby and amethyst eyes of anemones
Glow through me, fiercer than stars.
Flambeaux of earth, their dyes
From age-lost generations burn
Black soil, branches and mosses into light
That does not fail, though winter grip the rocks
To adamant. See, they come now
To lamp me through inscrutable dusk
And down the catacombs of death.

# ALLEN CURNOW

## From *Trees, Effigies, Moving Objects*

*eight*

### The Kitchen Cupboard

Sun, moon, and tides.
With the compliments of the *New Zealand Herald*
and Donaghy's Industries Limited makers
of the finest cordage since 1876.
Look on the inside of the cupboard door,
the middle one, on the left of the sink-bench.

All the bays are empty, a quick-drying wind
from the south-west browns the grey silt
the ebb-tide printed sexily, opulently,
making Nature's *art nouveau*, little as it matters
to mudlarking crabs and the morning's blue heron.

Olive, olive-budded, mangroves wait for the turn,
little as it means, to call that waiting.

A green car follows a blue car passing a brown car
on the Shore Road beyond the mangroves which wait
no more than the tide does because nothing waits.
Everything happens at once. It is enough.

That is not to say there is nothing to cry about,
only that the poetry of tears is a dead cuckoo.

The middle one, on the left of the sink-bench.
I stuck it on with cellotape. Not quite straight.

*ten*

### A Framed Photograph

The renaissance was six months old.

All the Kennedys were living at that time.
Jackie was hanging pictures in the White House.
*I figured he could use the experience*, Jack hornered,
*when he starts in legal practice*, naming Bobby
for Attorney-General.

Act one, scene one,
of the bloody melodrama. Everyone listened
while everyone read his poems. *BANG! BANG!*
and we cried all the way to My Lai.

To be silverly framed,
stood on the Bechstein, dusted daily
by the Jamaican girl whose eyes refuse them,
seeing alien Friendship one prolonged avenue
infinitely dusted, is a destiny which simply,
silverly they walk towards, towards my chair,
what jaunty pair
smiling the air
that flutters their trousers on Capitol Hill?
Why, Hiroshima Harry and the dandy Dean,
dust free. Heavenly muse!
fresh up your drink and sing.

What, exactly,
did he do at the Pentagon? He guessed he was
a deputy assistant secretary of defence,
*a political appointment*, modestly confided.
Hospitably home at cocktail time he took
one careful gin and tonic, excused himself
to mind State papers.

Dust the Bechstein, Anna.
Dust the megagothic national cathedral.
Dust destiny.

Fresh up. There is plenty of ice.

*Receptacle, receive me.*

## This Beach can be Dangerous

The fatalities of his nature cannot be disentangled
from the fatality of all that which has been and will
be. – NIETZSCHE

*WARNING*

They came back, a well known face
familiarly transfigured, lifelikeness only
cancer, coronary, burning, mutilation
could have bestowed, they came by millions
and a friend or two calling me by my name
and my father, by a name no other could know.

*BATHE BETWEEN THE FLAGS*

Each with the same expression, his own,
mirrored in the sand or the mind, came back
the way they went calling like winter waves
pick-a-back on the humped horizon they rode
the strong disturbed westerly airstream
which covered the North Island.

*DO NOT BATHE ALONE*

It was their company that made it possible
for me to walk there, cracking the odd shell
with the butt of a manuka stick,
happy to the point of hopelessness.


From *An Incorrigible Music*

*Canst Thou Draw Out Leviathan with an Hook*

I

An old Green River knife had to be scraped

of blood rust, scales, the dulled edge scrubbed
with a stone to the decisive whisper of steel
on the lips of the wooden grip.

You now have a cloud in your hand
hung blue dark over the waves and edgewise
luminous, made fast by the two brass rivets
keeping body and blade together, leaving
the other thumb free for feeling
how the belly will be slit and the spine severed.

The big kahawai had to swim close
to the rocks which kicked at the waves
which kept on coming steeply steaming,
wave overhanging wave
in a strong to gale offshore wind.

The rocks kicked angrily, the rocks
hurt only themselves, the seas without a scratch
made out to be storming and shattering,
but it was all an act that they ever broke
into breakers or even secretively
raged like the rocks, the wreckage of the land,
the vertigo, the self-lacerating
hurt of the land.
                              Swimming closer
the kahawai drew down the steely cloud
and the lure, the line you cast
from cathedral rock, the thoughtful death
whispering to the thoughtless,

*Will you be caught?*


II


Never let them die of the air,
pick up your knife and drive it
through the gills with a twist,

let the blood run fast,
quick bleeding makes best eating.


### III


An insult in the form of an apology
is the human answer to the inhuman
which rears up green roars down white,
and to the fish which is fearless:

if anyone knows a better it is a man
willing to abstain from his next breath,
who will not be found fishing from these rocks
but likeliest fished from the rip,

white belly to wetsuit black, swung copular
under the winching chopper's bubble,
too late for vomiting salt but fluent at last
in the languages of the sea.


### IV


A rockpool catches the blood,
so that in a red cloud of itself
the kahawai lies white belly uppermost.

Scales will glue themselves to the rusting blade
of a cloud hand–uppermost in the rockpool.


### V


Fingers and gobstick fail,
the hook's fast in the gullet,
the barb's behind the root
of the tongue and the tight
fibre is tearing the mouth

and you're caught, mate, you're caught,
the harder you pull it
the worse it hurts, and it makes
no sense whatever in the air
or the seas or the rocks
how you kick or cry, or sleeplessly
dream as you drown.

*A big one! a big one!*


## A Balanced Bait in Handy Pellet Form

Fluent in all the languages dead or living,
the sun comes up with a word of worlds all spinning
in a world of words, the way the mountain answers
to its name and that's the east and the sea *das meer,*
*la mer, il mare Pacifico*, and I am on my way to school

barefoot in frost beside the metalled road
which is beside the railway beside the water-race,
all spinning into the sun and all exorbitantly
expecting the one and identical, the concentric,
as the road, the rail, the water, and the bare feet run

eccentric to each other. Torlesse, no less,
first mountain capable of ice, joined the pursuit,
at its own pace revolved in a wintry blue
foot over summit, snow on each sunlit syllable,
taught speechless world-word word-world's ABC.

Because light is manifest by what it lights,
ladder-fern, fingernail, the dracophyllums
have these differing opacities, translucencies;
mown grass diversely parched is a skinned 'soul'
which the sun sloughed; similarly the spectral purples

perplexing the drab of the dugover topsoil
explain themselves too well to be understood.
There's no warmth here. The heart pulsates
to a tune of its own, and if unisons happen
how does anybody know? Dead snails

have left shells, trails, baffled epigraphy
and excreta of such slow short lives,
cut shorter by the pellets I 'scatter freely',
quick acting, eccentric to exorbitant flourishes
of shells, pencillings, drab or sunlit things

dead as you please, or as the other poet says,
*Our life is a false nature 'tis not in*
*the harmony of things.* There we go again, worrying
the concentric, the one and identical, to the bone
that's none of ours, eccentric to each other.

Millions die miserably never before their time.
The news comes late. Compassion sings to itself.
I read the excreta of all species, I write
a world as good as its word, active ingredient
30 g/kg (3%) Metaldehyde, in the form of a pellet.

### Dichtung und Wahrheit

A man I know wrote a book about a man he knew
and this man, or so he the man I know said, fucked
and murdered a girl to save her from the others
who would have fucked and murdered this girl
much more painfully and without finer feelings,
for letting the Resistance down and herself be fucked
by officers of the army of occupation, an oblation
sweet-smelling to Mars and equally to porn god
        Priapus.

What a fucking shame, this man the one the man
I know knew decided, if you want a job done well

do it yourself, and he did and he left her in a bath
of blood from the hole in her neck which he carved
in soldierly fashion, a way we have in the commandos,
after the fuck he knew she didn't of course
was her last, and a far far better thing, wasn't it?
than the bloody fuckup it would have been if he'd left
          her
to be unzipped and jack-the-rippered by a bunch
of scabby patriots with no regimental pride.

And he had this idea, and he mopped up the mess
and he laid her out naked on a bed with a crucifix
round her neck for those bastards the others
the sods to find, furious it must have made them.
And the man I know who knew this man or some
          other
man who did never forgot this fucking story,
it wouldn't leave him alone till he'd shown this goon
who actually did or said he did or was said to have
          done
the fucking deed what a better educated man
would have done and thought in his place.
And he wrote this book.

Experience like that, he exclaimed,
thrown away on a semiliterate whose English
was so imperfect you could hardly be certain
that what he did and what he said were connected,
let alone, by no fault of his own,
ignorant of the literature on the subject.
What can you do, with nothing but a cock
and a knife and a cuntful of cognac,
if you haven't got the talent?

*A big one!*

### Bring Your Own Victim

#### I

For Isaac the ram,
    for Iphigeneia the goat,
under the knife in the nick
    was the substitute.

The rule was never to notice
    what had taken place
by the sea, in the thicket, the thing
    was your sacrifice.

Agamemnon didn't inquire
    nor did Abraham,
would the highest settle for a goat
    or oblige with a ram?

The heavens might be humane
    but you never knew,
you sharpened your knife, you did
    what they said to do.

#### II

History began to be true
    at a later time.
The gods got into the act
    and they played our game.

You killed your mother because
    they said you had to,
and before the agon was over you knew
    you must have been mad to.

Bring your own victim
    ruled from then on,

conscience cut its milk teeth
  on the live bone.

Brutus knew that the blood
  had to be Caesar's,
Caiaphas and Pilate found
  no proxy for Jesus.

You sharpened your knife, you steeled
  yourself, the wound
twisted the knife in the hand,
  the knife in the mind.

Man or beast you bought
  on the hoof hung dead,
neither the cloud nor the covert sun
  commented,

and you never knew
  what hung by the other hook
in the heart, your blessed sacrifice
  or your damned mistake.

### III

You stood with an altar
  at your back, the grave
at your feet, no substitute offering
  to burn, wave, or heave.

You knew there was never nothing
  miracles wouldn't fix,
alone with your life, alone
  with your politics;

alive, alone, one-upping
  war, pestilence, famine,
happy in your Jonestowns, Hiroshimas,

happy to be human,

happy to be history
    in a galaxy of your own
among the spitting and the shitting stars
    alive, alone.

Spillage of bird blood,
    fish, and flesh went,
the spoonful in the womb, the aged
    and incontinent,

under your steeled thumb:
    so to imagine
slaughterman, overman, everyman,
    time's eminent surgeon.


## An Incorrigible Music

It ought to be impossible to be mistaken
about these herons, to begin with
you can count them, it's been done successfully
with swans daffodils blind mice, any number
of dead heroes and heavenly bodies.

Eleven herons are not baked in porcelain,
helpless to hatch the credulities of art
or to change places, e.g. number seven
counting from the left with number five,
or augment themselves by number twelve arriving
over the mangroves. Thirteen, fourteen, fifteen,
punctually the picture completes itself
and is never complete.

           The air
and the water being identically still,
each heron is four herons,
one right-side-up in the air,

one up-side-down in the tide,
and these two doubled by looking at.

The mudbacked mirrors in your head
multiply the possibilities of human
error, but what's the alternative?

The small wind instruments in the herons' throats
play an incorrigible music on a scale
incommensurate with hautboys and baroque wigs.

There's only one book in the world, and that's the one
everyone accurately misquotes.

*A big one! A big one!*


## A Reliable Service

The world can end any time
it likes, say, 10.50 am
of a bright winter Saturday,

that's when the *Bay Belle*
casts off, the diesels are picking
up step, the boatmaster leans

to the wheel, the white water
shoves Paihia jetty back.
Nobody aboard but the two of us.

Fifteen minutes to Russell
was once upon a time
before, say, 10.50 am.

The ketch slogging seaward
off Kororàreka Point,
the ensign arrested in

mid–flap, are printed and
pinned on a wall at the end
of the world. No lunch

over there either, the place
at the beach is closed. The *Bay
Belle* is painted bright

blue from stem to stern.
She lifts attentively. That
will be all, I suppose.

### An Excellent Memory

Brasch wrote 'these islands' and I
'two islands', counting one short,
and 'the islands' in our language
were remoter, palmier Polynesian chartings,
a there for a here.
                    The cartographer
dots them in, the depth of his blue
denotes the depth of the entirely
surrounding water.
                    The natives,
given time, with the help of an atlas,
come to recognize in the features of
the coastline a face
of their own, a puzzled mirror
for a puzzling globe.
                    'Always in these
islands,' that was Charles Brasch
getting it right the very first time.

Pat Laking knew it by heart the whole sonnet
all the way down to 'Distance
looks our way', and it did,
over the martinis in Observatory Circle,
Washington DC, demanding by way

of an answering look nothing more
than an excellent memory.
                                    That was
8 November 1974, just about
midnight, give or take a few minutes.


## *You Will Know When You Get There*

Nobody comes up from the sea as late as this
in the day and the season, and nobody else goes down

the last steep kilometre, wet-metalled where
a shower passed shredding the light which keeps

pouring out of its tank in the sky, through summits,
trees, vapours thickening and thinning. Too

credibly by half celestial, the dammed
reservoir up there keeps emptying while the light lasts

over the sea, where it 'gathers the gold against
it'. The light is bits of crushed rock randomly

glinting underfoot, wetted by the short
shower, and down you go and so in its way does

the sun which gets there first. Boys, two of them,
turn campfirelit faces, a hesitancy to speak

is a hesitancy of the earth rolling back and away
behind this man going down to the sea with a bag

to pick mussels, having an arrangement with the tide,
the ocean to be shallowed three point seven metres,

one hour's light to be left, and there's the excrescent
moon sponging off the last of it. A door

slams, a heavy wave, a door, the sea-floor shudders.
Down you go alone, so late, into the surge-black
    fissure.

# KENDRICK SMITHYMAN

## *An Ordinary Day Beyond Kaitaia*

### 1

Cabbage tree heads, they nod,
profoundly confirmed,
towards a church's new white paint.

About midmorning an elementary
summer breeze arrives from the coast
too late to alter. The township has
already dedicated this day, to usage.
An old disorder yields, to wise men
who come from the south. Where was a stable,
they made the Tourist Inn; for shepherds,
a public convenience of concrete blocks,
the kind that's called hollowstone.

Fused with, confused as, memories,
assumed a means of tree pollens
or a shifty heat off the church's
dazzling corrugated roof,
inconstant air implicates farmlands
in a conspiracy of nation, utility,
populist myth. You must change
your life, Rilke's archaic Apollo urged.
They have done so. They have put by.
Between a sea and an ocean
the farmlands lie low
without a hill to comfort them.

A peasant people won hard
from waste, teaching their weird flats
a novel language, an old belief.
Saint Cyril and Saint Methodius
they pray for, but at the bridge
to the dairy factory at midmorning

those echoes which coil remember
a coast not broken or so far displaced,
just accommodated. You breathe
a last of ozone, of kelp iodine.
Like the popping of kelp on a drift
fire, you hear pods closer.

Between the soil, the sand, swamp
and sea, is an understanding.
To change your life you must understand
how your life goes, and where.


2


Like so many huntsmen
they move intently.
They have an assignation
with a wildfowl, garishly feathered,
a fowl of unearthly voice.
You have not seen her like.

Dear object, lulled in myth,
you may yet be splendid
as the firebird, birdwoman,
the snowbird, woman of white
fire
        though here the quarry, much
harried, burns away through heavy
scent down to the burning clay
under an overburden of flowers.

The wreaths are already wilting
and they are not yet out of town.
Today a myth dies a little more,
a little less than kind.
We are aliens.

3

And the kin: tanned, earnest
Slavic Polynesian faces,
all the men wearing dark
suits. Perhaps they are going
to a wedding beyond
the dairy factory.

Do not think so.
You must change your life.
As of now, you marry conflicting wishes.
You also will progress
towards the sunbaked slope,
being contracted. Hedged about
with hakea, you go. Bitterns nest
in a raupo swamp beside, harriers
stiffly tread its edge.
Archaic Apollo, your people,
they taught the vine to grow
wild along their roads. Clay
like talc, mica-sharp grits dust
the grapes' tight premature testicular
clusters. If the fruits will seed,
who will pick them over? They go
earth-borne. Hard, to discover
when they ripen. Hard to know,
the end due of their season.

On the west course to Tasman's sea
pine stumps, insignis, broken teeth.
Alien forests, made quick
to accommodate, sicken.
Go slowly, carefully, like those
who pick a path among stumps,
like the funeral cars in high
day, headlamps teasing on low beam.
My wife's dark glasses reflected
cars, lights, unreconciled twin suns.

4

They have put by

an earliest type washing-machine
several lawnmowers (hand and powered)
tables          deckchairs          beds

a 1911 Montgomery Ward mailorder catalogue
wirestrainers spanners crosscut saws
shark-repellents surfcasting rods
lifebuoys and a mae west (with whistle)
an almost complete household physician

they have put by in a colonial junkshop

ships' riding lamps,
verdigrised brass
horseless carriage lanterns,
bullseyes, hurricanes with bent
wires and no glass, their wicks
shrivelled, smoke blanked.

Fires banked, they see perpetually
nothing. Illustrate nothing.
Shelve them beside
fossil eggs by whale vertebrae
windwashed, seablown, beyond
whiteness hardly temporised
by the mere dust which they breed
or dust which is imported from their road
tending eastward to the Pacific

past garage, past creek
where fishermen compare. Turbid
weed congregates in the gut.

Changing, their lives' style.

5

Their river decayed,
but their soil learned new tricks
of speech, for winds of hay paddocks,
a dialect fitting herds,
a stress and accent of flocks and crops.

Why, if intensely assured
by confident highlights every
where present to trouble exposure,
should I sourly dawdle,
doodling mementoes, cryptically
muttering
        I go, thou goest, he/she/or it,
and one (impersonally) goes

If we live,
we go. You go. They, a common gender, go.

I am a stranger. Too facile, to say
We are all strangers. The land is made
to our liking. Not far north
they are going, to offer.

To Hine, whose likeness still the swamp.
To Hine-nui, whose tumultuous hair the chattering
      idiot cabbage trees mimic,
Hine-nui-te-Po, She who is darkness,
at the heart speaking of the land,
along the wind's edge, at the sea line.
You cannot put by. I write in her dust
on the bonnet of our station wagon
M A T E. That will do, for a time.

If we live, we stand in language.
You must change your words.

## Friday Night

How can you believe in it,
incredulous of truly available wealth
to cash in on, not affluence

yet at a same time, the very same
time, that Channel which may be worn
as far away as Easter Island is
putting a prayer shawl about any
shoulders wanting to get warmed by
tradition. One moon rising

has weeds offer themselves as
phylacteries for such who want,
our island over fishnet waters
like a book opens for such who want
to read. My friends of many
standing years,

this being Friday night all over
part of a world, are lighting candles
at their table, putting flames'
adroit flowers
in the mouth of wine glasses
which say the words after

his lights answering
her words and answering waters
at the same time. Which go making
sounds, like shawls falling.


## Resort

Indigo, chartreuse, tangerine, lollipop
madder and eau-de-nil. Also, conservative
white as virgins' napkins or their sheets,
and cutouts so blazingly citric

that mouths pucker without needing
to taste. Convocation
of triangles! every outer edge sharpened
by to and fro sawing at one midsummer
midday in passage full with
kids' voices more than seabirds',
grounded on the launching ramp.

Then lunge the tide, taking
flight upharbour, squadrons delta-
winged banking independently from buoy
to buoy. On the south coast stand
foursquare oblongs
which are hotels, simply redroofed
like those blocks which came in toy building sets –
or Noah's Ark red? Verandahs will have
to wrinkle their foreheads, screw up their eyes
if they want to see as far as we are
where trailers and cradles go
rank by rank agreeably
under the hill.

Like gulls they flash at channels.
They stake no fish. They round, for return
meeting face to face with
breezes which they must, if to survive,
outwit by snappy wheelings, unannounced
change in course, breaking step.

They serve without memory. Without doubt,
guiltless. *Dubito, ergo sum*
of this whole holiday sweating mangrove swamps,
cabbage tree prairies inland, an oceanic
upcountry of pig fern. Shall I buy you
a popsicle, a jelly topper, a vanilla cone –
would you like that, just something plain?

The triangles are swinging, precisely.
Their intentions make clear.

They march as though ceremony committed them
over that part of the harbour where lie
ribs with keelbone, ligaments of the whaler
massacred. Burned, it's been stripped in
every textbook. Towards evening
Taratara's shade will dive like a gannet
near that implicit water. What will
the dinghies do then?


### The Last Moriori

Reputedly last of his kind,
quite surely one of the last
not crossbred but (as They said) pure
as pure goes, a Chatham Island Moriori
taken for a slave when a boy, taken
again in some other raiding, passed
from band to band, from place to place
until he washed up on the River.
That was the story, anyway, which is
as may be. He was

very old, he did not belong,
some chunk of totara which lay too long
    in acid swamp.
He was kumara left on the pit's floor,
    sweetness dried, its hulk drawn small.
He was what you found in caves but did not
    mention, travesty gone
beyond human. A tatty topcoat, bowler hat,
blanket which seemed to look your way
without seeing you from the stoop of a hut
at the Pa. A few weak hungers,
he survived. He endured,

already myth, beyond legends of his kind,
a poor fact. But the fact was, and the myth
was, and they endure together.

This is written particularly to you.
Remembering, I shiver again as on that day
taking small comfort from our day as it is.

# HONE TUWHARE

*Ron Mason*

Time has pulled up a chair, dashed
a stinging litre from a jug of wine.
My memory is a sluggard.

I reject your death, but can't dismiss it.
For it was never an occasion for woman
sobs and keenings: your stoic-heart

would not permit it. And that calcium–covered
pump had become a sudden road–block bringing
heavy traffic to a tearing halt.

Your granite–words remain.
Austere fare, but nonetheless adequate for the
honest sustenance they give.

And for myself, a challenge.
A preoccupation now more intensely felt, to tilt
a broken *taiaha* inexpertly

to my old lady, Hine–nui–o–te–Po, bless the old
bitch: shrewd guardian of that infrequent *duende*
that you and Lorca knew about, playing hard–to–get.

Easy for you now, man. You've joined your literary
ancestors, whilst I have problems still in finding
mine, lost somewhere

in the confusing swirl, now thick now thin,
Victoriana-Missionary fog hiding legalized land-rape
and gentlemen thugs. Never mind, you've taught me

confidence and ease in dredging for my own
        bedraggled
myths, and you bet: weighing the China experience

yours and mine. They balance.

Your suit has not the right cut for me except around
the gut. I'll keep the jacket though: dry-cleaned
it'll absorb new armpit sweat.

*Ad Dorotheum*: She and I together found the poem
you'd left for her behind a photograph.

> *Lest you be a dead man's*
> > *slave*
>
> *Place a branch upon the*
> > *grave*
>
> *Nor allow your term of*
> > *grief*
>
> *To pass the fall of its last*
> > *leaf*

'Bloody Ron, making up to me,' she said, quickly:
too quickly.

But Time impatient, creaks a chair. And from the
jug I pour sour wine to wash away the only land
I own, and that between the toes.

A red libation to your good memory, friend. There's
work yet, for the living.

## *A Burnt Offering to your Greenstone Eyes,* Tangaroa

When I go, Earth, I shall not succumb
to your pervasive clutch:

nor forbear the sun's hot licks,
or ribbed umbrella of rain slanting.

I'll not crouch there to the lee-side;
sit lonely in the shadow of the wind.

Burnt and sere, my soul on ashen wings
shall dust instead the leaning

greenstone walls of *Tangaroa* advancing,
crumbling . . .

*Ah, then watch him froth and gag, Earth.*
*Watch him heave!*

## Snowfall

It didn't make a grand entrance and I nearly
missed it – tip-toeing up on me as it did when
I was half asleep and suddenly, they're there
before my eyes – white pointillist flakes on
a Hotere canvas – swirling about on untethered

gusts of air and spreading thin uneven
thicknesses of white snow-cover on drooping
ti-kouka leaves, rata, a lonely kauri, pear
and beech tree. Came without hesitation right
inside my opened window licking my neck, my

arms, my nose as I leaned far out to embrace
a phantom sky above the house-tops and over
the sea: *Hey, where's the horizon? I shall*
*require a boat, you know – two strong arms?*
. . . and snow, kissing and lipping my face

gently, mushily, like a pet whale, or (if
you prefer) a shark with red bite – sleet
sting hot as ice. Well,
it's stopped now. Stunning sight. Unnerved,
the birds have stopped singing, tucking their

beaks under warm armpits: temporarily. And for
miles upon whitened miles around, there is no
immediate or discernible movement except from

me, transfixed, and moved by an interior
agitation – an armless man applauding.

*Bravo*, I whisper. *Bravissimo*. Standing ovation.
Why not . . . Oh, come in, Spring.

## LOUIS JOHNSON

### *How to Measure a Cat*

A year in the life of a cat equates
with a decade in your own. This sleek
supine example asleep at my heater while
I pause, pent over words and the ordering
of life into manageable measures, is in
that interesting late-adolescence I so burned
through alert and hoping; but, being governed
by a more cutting logic, is not
in the same danger of blotting a copybook;
may even wear better.
                                    For me, fear
was the surgeon that cauterized risk and often
sat at the top of the fence to italicize
lyrics yowled at the moon – that goddess
padding the mists, single-eyed and sailing
Cycloptic seas of dreams full-bellying.


To steal dreams may be to plunder all, but
there's arithmetic of other kinds to live by.
Three meals a day to count from; fingers and toes
for those whose years are decades and whose urgings
madden as seas, waters and blood respond
to reasonable gravity.
                                    This one is freed of ambition –
a true companion – and will not fight
for a place in the world or the sixty-nines of position.
Content is often to be without content
and life a pun inscribed with a knife.
                                    I measure all
by words inched over tricky pages. The cat
measures me by provision (kidneys and blade steak
cut on the crossgrain), and comes to kitchen sounds
of sharpening knives. Aversion therapy fails
in the face of a true addiction. You cannot
convert a cat to Christ though love may prove

both its, and your, undoing. Sense how its engine
whirrs into rhyme out of instinct: recognize how
your decayed and ageing motor stirs into fitful gear
sighting beauty, sensing danger.
                              Prompted, cats
move like quicksilver, gauge the weathers of love,
their sinuous silhouettes serve
as barometers, define like mirrors.

### Coming and Going

If love is what would make one offer himself
to bear the pains of another, there is so much
the baby does not understand I would gladly
stand in her stead for. But you cannot take
the pang for another or teach
pain quicker than the piercing thorn
any more than explain to the blind
the colour of blood or a bird.

Through glass of the kitchen door she watches
me return through the burning light of the day
and the indescribable sunset; her arms
suddenly wild signalling welcome.
What she makes of my comings and goings
I cannot guess or begin to explain.
Here one minute, gone another: small wonder
children find fathers incomprehensible
shadows, moon-ruled like tides, undependable.

Which is not why I pick her up from the floor –
but to secure for myself the fact of return
and the weight of the welcome. My fifty-odd
years are so close to a last departure
I know I should have thought harder
about such a new beginning. I tell myself
that love is quite as extreme as any entrance
or exit, and does not come too late. Its colour
glows in the room where I have closed the door.

## This Particular Christian

This particular Christian driving home from church,
euphoric and consoled, has not attended
well enough to his articles of belief,
shown care for the feathers of detail falling
(banana-skins at the top of the stair; the bump,
in the unmended road where it narrows
to hug the coastal cliffs), and is suddenly strung
on the high wire of the skid. It could be anyone,
not this particular Christian taken unguarded,
his throat contracting to climb the high note
of the rewinding anthem that causes the spin
(he straining to praise as wheels unguided burn
over the roadcrown), and the boy blown broken
backwards into not caring; and caring too much
the broken-throated cry of the woman smashing the
        near horizon.

# LAURIS EDMOND

## Commercial Traveller

Dinner's over. Now he mumbles at
his cigarette, summons the waiter,
scoffs the last fine
sticky drops of wine. 'That's better –
damn good in fact. Now coffee
with a touch – here, boy – a smack
of Benedictine.' The sweet fire dives
down, but prudently he thinks to peck
back from the tray his extra ten cent
piece (he'll be on the road
tomorrow, no more favours thanks
from this fellow). Now his head
settles grunting back
into copious ease, armchair deep;
the stale public smells lounge
away; he blows smoke rings, a drop
of gravy blots his waistcoat. Inside
his heart waits, famished – no friends come
to talk to greedy boy.
Let him suck his thumb.

## 3 A. M.

I remember the last red rose
and that it darkened a little
every day, drawing into itself
almost black at the end in its
bright green bottle
on the white sill by the kitchen window,
and the winter weather waning
the garden greening, beyond –
I remember it died, months ago.

The last hard clasp of hands
and the standing together
in the blue winter twilight
with infinite gentleness talking
inconsequentially through
someone's silent weeping – that too
is over; we scattered long ago
to our afternoon houses
to work and to sleep.

But the night is querulous and full
of arrangements; composing
answers to letters, remembering
obligations, I am held as
at a dull meeting; dry-eyed,
tired-minded, I hear no voices
but the night wind
meddling at the silence.

In a great sorrow we are helpless:
children, we trust the pitiless stars
to lead us by the hand; this small
darkness is a shut room.
It is not pain we fear, but triviality.


From *Wellington Letter*

## XI

There are fixed points
like stars; they wake each night
after days of flux and we say
'this is love'. It is not so easy –
to hold your frail poise
you must stand against me;
when the lout comes in to the room
you must leave and speak to him.

This shaggy brute must follow us
into the moonlight where we walk
distracted under the jagged galaxies.
On the icy grass by the precipice
it will be his selfish insistence
that mortifies and saves us.

## Three Women

Green the drawn curtains, the walls,
the very air is green where our
discovered words uncurl new tendrils.
Exile? Yes of course we talk of it,
meaning different things.

Yours, familiar, stands before
your house in full leaf; through it
you glimpse chimney pots and spires.
My startled reappraisals struggle,
needing time to root and grow.

The lamplight's clear pool gravely
reflects our difference, our likeness.
You pour Dutch gin from a terra cotta
jar; we speak of home as children
there might speak of England.

Morning light is harsher; in the early
train a woman sits rigid, her whole
body clenched yet helpless to hold
the tears that cover her face . . .
black, among the English newspapers.

## Town Ghost

After the rain
came the town ghost

eyes like street lamps
yellow sulphurous
fists big boulders
coat black in the wind
strode past the wharves
round into Cable Street
shoved aside spectres
warehouse porters
flower auctioneers
aching with injury
silently bawling
when I came up
spat on the asphalt
*Look lady just don't*
*you interfere.*


## A Difficult Adjustment

It takes time, and there are setbacks;
on Monday, now, you were all ennui
and malice; but this morning I am
pleased with my handiwork: your
stick figure moves, your two eyes
are large and dark enough, your
expression is conveniently mild.
You have begun to disagree with me,
but weakly, so that I can easily prove
you wrong. In fact you are entirely
satisfactory.
            I suppose, really, you are
dead. But someone silently lies down
with me at night and shows a soothing
tenderness. I have killed the pain
of bone and flesh; I suffer no laughter
now, nor hear the sound of troubled
voices speaking in the dark.

## Love Poem

Everything will happen. Your friend
will go to Paris, my uncle give up
at last his dreams of wild horses
flying over the hills of his boyhood
farm; that quaking marriage will break.

We do not speak of ourselves, but as
we walk down the stairs snow falls,
coming to lay soft stars on the dark
tweed of our hearts. We brush away for
each other the little messages of death.

In the street there are two young men
exuberantly quarrelling; we pass slowly,
close together and carefully keeping
in step. It is as though we have
something very light and fragile to carry.

## The Names

Six o'clock, the morning still and
the moon up, cool profile of the night;
time small and flat as an envelope –
see, you slip out easily: do I know you?
Your names have still their old power,
they sing softly like voices across water.

Virginia Frances Martin Rachel Stephanie
Katherine – the sounds blend and chant
in some closed chamber of the ear, poised
in the early air before echoes formed.
Suddenly a door flies open, the music
breaks into a roar, it is everywhere;

now it's laughter and screaming, the crack
of a branch in the plum tree, the gasping

and blood on the ground; it is sea–surge
and summer, 'Watch me!' sucked under
the breakers; the hum of the lupins, through
sleepy popping of pods the saying of names.

And all the time the wind that creaked in
the black macrocarpas and whined in the wires
was waiting to sweep us away; my children who
were my blood and breathing I do not know you:
we are friends, we write often, there are
occasions, news from abroad. One of you is dead.

I do not listen fearfully for you in the night,
exasperating you with my concern,
I scarcely call this old habit love –
yet you have come to me this white morning,
and remind me that to name a child is brave,
or foolhardy; even now it shakes me.

The small opaque moon, wafer of light,
grows fainter and disappears; but
the names will never leave me, I hear
them calling like boatmen far over
the harbour at first light. They will sound
in the dreams of your children's children.

### Going to Moscow

The raspberries they gave us for dessert
were delicious, sharp-tasting and furry,
served in tiny white bowls; you spooned
cream on to mine explaining I'd find it sour.
The waitress with huge eyes, and a tuft
of hair pinched like a kewpie, so wanted
to please us she dropped two plates
as she swooped through the kitchen door.
No one could reassure her. Snow was falling,
when you spoke, across the narrow white

cloth I could scarcely hear for the distance
nor see you through floating drifts.

Then the tall aunt brought out her dog,
a small prickly sprig like a toy; we put on
our coats and in the doomed silence Chekhov
the old master nodded at us from the wings.
At the last my frozen lips would not
kiss you, I could do nothing but talk
to the terrible little dog; but you stood
still, your polished shoes swelling up
like farm boots. There are always some
who must stay in the country when others
are going to Moscow. Your eyes were
a dark lake bruised by the winter trees.

# ALISTAIR CAMPBELL

## The Dark Lord of Savaiki

*I am the one in your dreams,*
*master of passion,*
*favourite child*
*of Tumu and Papauri.*
                    Te Ara o Tumu


### I

### Under the Tamanu Tree

Who, who and who?
Who is the dark Lord of Savaiki?
        Crab castings,
                convulsions under the house
where the landcrabs
        tell their grievances
to the roots of the tamanu tree.
Agitation of the leaves,
        the palm trees clash
                        their fronds,
and the wind hurries past
        clutching in its fingers
the leaf-wrapped souls
        of children torn
                from the eyelids
of despairing mothers.
                        Hung
on spiderwebs for safekeeping,
        they will dangle there,
until the spirits come
                and eat them.


### II

### The Witch of Hanoa

When Kavatai died,

his son Paroa, as chief mourner,
wrapped his corpse in mats
and hung it from the ceiling
    to decay in decent isolation,
neighbour to the stars
                and the grieving wind
that rode the rooftree
                for three months
and terrified Te Tautua people
    with its groans
                and high-pitched whistling.
All this time,
                his widow Puatama,
feared throughout the kingdom
    for her sorcery,
fed his spirit at her breast
            until it grew so vast
it burst apart the ribcage
    of the house,
                a monstrous storm
that tore up trees
    and levelled villages,
                rampaging
to the west as far as Manihiki.
Her grief assuaged,
    she called his spirit back,
as she would a dangerous child,
and, chastened,
    he returned
                upon a mango's back
and beached at Hanoa,
where he lies in peace
    with Puatama
                in an unmarked grave.

### III

#### Teu

Mother, you were there
    at the passage
        when our ship arrived.
The sea, heavy as oil,
    heaved unbroken
           on the reef,
the stars
    lay in clusters
        on the water,
and you wept
    when you laid
        the Southern Cross
upon our eyes.

### IV

#### At Nahe

At Nahe, attended by a sandshark,
    I waded in the shallows
that seemed as white and pure
        as happiness,
    or the shark itself.
I was happy being a child again,
    and, careless as a child
        in a treasure house,
I ripped up chunks of coral
    to take home.
        Horrid amputation!
The living creatures seemed
        to shriek,
and bled a kind of ichor.

## VII

### Brother Shark

The black mango
                is a priest
in his marae
                of blazing coral
where Ataranga's sunken house
        tilts
                towards Savaiki
and the setting sun.


## VIII

### Omoka

It will be like this one day
        when I sail home to die –
the boat crunching up on to the sand,
then wading through warm water
                        to the beach,
the friendly voices
        round me in the darkness,
the sky dying out
        behind the trees of Omoka,
                and reaching out of hands.


## IX

### Trade Winds

You were just a girl,
        one of two wild sisters,
when he came to Tongareva,
                his soul eaten away
by five years

in the trenches.
You followed him
from island to island,
bore his children
only to see your dreams
break up
on the hidden reef
of Savaiki.
Mother,
your footsteps falter
outside my window,
where you have waited
fifty years
for your children
to return.
The moon comes out,
lovely
as a mother's face
over a sleeping child.
The trade winds
are your fingers
on my eyelids.


X

Bosini's Tomb

Ancestral shapes
on the beach,
lying beside their drawn-up boats,
chatting and laughing softly
as they await the dawn —
so many names to remember,
so many names to honour!
Grandfather Bosini,
why do you beckon
from the deeper shadows
beyond your tomb?

The children of Marata
                    join hands
with the children of Tumu
and have peaceful dreams.
                    They smile to see
Father and Mother
          walking hand in hand
across the swirling waters
                    of Taruia Passage,
where the leaping dolphins
          celebrate the dawn.

# JAMES K. BAXTER

## From *Jerusalem Sonnets*

### (Poems for Colin Durning)

1

The small grey cloudy louse that nests in my beard
Is not, as some have called it, 'a pearl of God' –

No, it is a fiery tormentor
Waking me at two a.m.

Or thereabouts, when the lights are still on
In the houses in the pa, to go across thick grass

Wet with rain, feet cold, to kneel
For an hour or two in front of the red flickering

Tabernacle light – what He sees inside
My meandering mind I can only guess –

A madman, a nobody, a raconteur
Whom He can joke with – 'Lord,' I ask Him,

'Do You or don't You expect me to put up with lice?'
His silent laugh still shakes the hills at dawn.


18

Yesterday I planted garlic,
Today, sunflowers – 'the non-essentials first'

Is a good motto – but these I planted in honour of
The Archangel Michael and my earthly friend,

Illingworth, Michael also, who gave me the seeds –

And they will turn their wild pure golden discs

Outside my bedroom, following Te Ra
Who carries fire for us in His terrible wings

(Heresy, man!) – and if He wanted only
For me to live and die in this old cottage,

It would be enough, for the angels who keep
The very stars in place resemble most

These green brides of the sun, hopelessly in love with
Their Master and Maker, drunkards of the sky.


## 35

The trap I am setting to catch a tribe
Is all but furnished – on Friday Father Condon

Will (if he remembers) bring from Ohakune
The crucifix my friend Milton carved

With its garments made of wood shavings
And a faceless face, Maori or pakeha either

As the light catches it; also the workman Buddha
Hoani lent me, and the Hindu image of Mara

Trix handed on so as to be wholly poor –
What else, Colin? They say it is best

To break a rotten egg in the creek
To get eels – I think I am that egg

And Te Ariki must crack me open
If the fish are to be drawn in at all.

### 36

Brother Ass, Brother Ass, you are full of fancies,
You want this and that – a woman, a thistle,

A poem, a coffeebreak, a white bed, no crabs;
And now you complain of the weight of the Rider

Who will set you free to gallop in the light of the sun!
Ah well, kick Him off then, and see how you go

Lame-footed in the brambles; your disconsolate bray
Is ugly in my ears – long ago, long ago,

The battle was fought and the issue decided
As to who would be King – go on, little donkey

Saddled and bridled by the Master of the world,
Be glad you can distinguish not an inch of the track,

That the stones are sharp, that your hide can itch,
That His true weight is heavy on your back.

### 37

Colin, you can tell my words are crippled now;
The bright coat of art He has taken away from me

And like the snail I crushed at the church door
My song is my stupidity;

The words of a homely man I cannot speak,
Home and bed He has taken away from me;

Like an old horse turned to grass I lift my head
Biting at the blossoms of the thorn tree;

Prayer of priest or nun I cannot use,

The songs of His house He has taken away from me;

As blind men meet and touch each other's faces
So He is kind to my infirmity;

As the cross is lifted and the day goes dark
Rule over myself He has taken away from me.

## The Ikons

Hard, heavy, slow, dark,
Or so I find them, the hands of Te Whaea

Teaching me to die. Some lightness will come later
When the heart has lost its unjust hope

For special treatment. Today I go with a bucket
Over the paddocks of young grass,

So delicate like fronds of maidenhair,
Looking for mushrooms. I find twelve of them,

Most of them little, and some eaten by maggots,
But they'll do to add to the soup. It's a long time now

Since the great ikons fell down,
God, Mary, home, sex, poetry,

Whatever one uses as a bridge
To cross the river that only has one beach,

And even one's name is a way of saying –
'This gap inside a coat' – the darkness I call God,

The darkness I call Te Whaea, how can they translate
The blue calm evening sky that a plane tunnels through

Like a little wasp, or the bucket in my hand,

Into something else? I go on looking

For mushrooms in the field, and the fist of longing
Punches my heart, until it is too dark to see.


### He Waiata mo Te Kare

#### 1

Up here at the wharepuni
That star at the kitchen window
Mentions your name to me.

Clear and bright like running water
It glitters above the rim of the range,
You in Wellington,
I at Jerusalem,

Woman, it is my wish
Our bodies should be buried in the same grave.


#### 2

To others my love is a plaited kono
Full or empty,
With chunks of riwai,
Meat that stuck to the stones.

To you my love is a pendant
Of inanga greenstone,
Too hard to bite,
Cut from a boulder underground.

You can put it in a box
Or wear it over your heart.

One day it will grow warm,

One day it will tremble like a bed of rushes
And say to you with a man's tongue,
'Taku ngakau ki a koe!'


### 3

I have seen at evening
Two ducks fly down
To a pond together.

The whirring of their wings
Reminded me of you.


### 4

At the end of our lives
Te Atua will take pity
On the two whom he divided.

To the tribe he will give
Much talking, te pia and a loaded
      hangi.

To you and me he will give
A whare by the seashore
Where you can look for crabs and kina
And I can watch the waves
And from time to time see your face
With no sadness,
Te Kare o Nga Wai.


### 5

No rafter paintings,
No grass-stalk panels,
No Maori mass,

Christ and his Mother
Are lively Italians
Leaning forward to bless,

No taniko band on her head,
No feather cloak on his shoulder,

No stairway to heaven,
No tears of the albatross.

Here at Jerusalem
After ninety years
Of bungled opportunities,
I prefer not to invite you
Into the pakeha church.


6


Waves wash on the beaches.
They leave a mark for only a minute.
Each grey hair in my beard
Is there because of a sin,

The mirror shows me
An old tuatara,
He porangi, he tutua,
Standing in his dusty coat.

I do not think you wanted
Some other man.

I have walked barefoot from the tail of the fish to the
        nose
To say these words.

7

Hilltop behind hilltop,
A mile of green pungas
In the grey afternoon
Bow their heads to the slanting spears of rain.

In the middle room of the wharepuni
Kat is playing the guitar, –
'Let it be! Let it be!'

Don brings home a goat draped round his shoulders.
Tonight we'll eat roasted liver.

One day, it is possible,
Hoani and Hilary might join me here,
Tired of the merry-go-round.

E hine, the door is open,
There's a space beside me.


8

Those we knew when we were young,
None of them have stayed together,
All their marriages battered down like trees
By the winds of a terrible century.

I was a gloomy drunk.
You were a troubled woman.
Nobody would have given tuppence for our chances,
Yet our love did not turn to hate.

If you could fly this way, my bird,
One day before we both die,
I think you might find a branch to rest on.

I chose to live in a different way.

Today I cut the grass from the paths
With a new sickle,
Working till my hands were blistered.

I never wanted another wife.


9


Now I see you conquer age
As the prow of a canoe beats down
The plumes of Tangaroa.

You, straight-backed, a girl,
Your dark hair on your shoulders,
Lifting up our grandchild,

How you put them to shame,
All the flouncing girls!

Your face wears the marks of age
As a warrior his moko,
Double the beauty,
A soul like the great albatross

Who only nests in mid ocean
Under the eye of Te Ra.

You have broken the back of age.
I tremble to see it.


10


Taraiwa has sent us up a parcel of smoked eels
With skins like fine leather.
We steam them in the colander.
He tells us the heads are not for eating,

So I cut off two heads
And throw them out to Archibald,
The old tomcat. He growls as he eats
Simply because he's timid.

Earlier today I cut thistles
Under the trees in the graveyard,
And washed my hands afterwards,
Sprinkling the sickle with water.

That's the life I lead,
Simple as a stone,
And all that makes it less than good, Te Kare,
Is that you are not beside me.


## From *Autumn Testament*

### 15

The creek has to run muddy before it can run clear!
Here in this very room I have seen it happen,

The lads and the girls in chairs, some kneeling, some
    standing,
Some wearing headbands, one strumming the guitar,

And Father Theodore setting down an old
Packing case covered with a blanket

For the altar of his Mass. There was no wind
To burst the house door in, no tongues of fire,

But new skin under wounds, the Church becoming
    human,
As if religion were not the cemetery of hope

But a flowering branch – ah well, it was some time
    ago,

Sly is in jail under a two-year sentence,

Manu has gone back to the ward at Porirua,
And the Church can count her losses in Pharisaic peace.


19


The bodies of the young are not the flower,
As some may imagine – it is the soul

Struggling in an iron net of terror
To become itself, to learn to love well,

To nourish the Other – when Mumma came from
    the bin
With scars from the wrist to the shoulder,

They combed her hair and put their arms around her
Till she began to blossom. The bread she baked for
    us

Was better kai than you'd get in a restaurant
Because her soul was in it. The bread we share in
    the churches

Contains a Christ nailed up in solitude,
And all our pain is to be crystal vases,

As if the mice were afraid of God the cat
Who'd plunge them into Hell for touching one
    another.


22


To pray for an easy heart is no prayer at all
Because the heart itself is the creaking bridge

On which we cross these Himalayan gorges

From bluff to bluff. To sweat out the soul's blood

Midnight after midnight is the ministry of Jacob,
And Jacob will be healed. This body that shivers

In the foggy cold, tasting the sour fat,
Was made to hang like a sack on its thief's cross,

Counting it better than bread to say the words of
    Christ,
'*Eli! Eli!*' The Church will be shaken like a

Blanket in the wind, and we are the fleas that fall
To the ground for the dirt to cover. Brother thief,

You who are lodged in my ribcage, do not rail at
The only gate we have to paradise.


### 29

I think the Lord on his axe-chopped cross
Is laughing as usual at my poems,

My solemn metaphors, my ladder-climbing dreams,
For he himself is incurably domestic,

A family man who never lifted a sword,
An only son with a difficult mother,

If you understand my thought. He has saddled me
    again
With the cares of a household, and no doubt

Has kept me away from Otaki
Because I'd spout nonsense, and wear my poverty

As a coat of vanity. Down at the Mass
Today, as Francie told me to, I took Communion

For her (and Siân as well) cursing gently
The Joker who won't let me shuffle my own pack.


32


Life can be a hassle. Are you free of it, Monsignor,
While you dispute the changes of the liturgy

Or polish up your golf style? At one p.m.
Either in your house or my house

The soul may plunge into pain like a child who slides
Through the grass at the lip of a mine-shaft,

Therefore don't ask me, 'What do you mean by that
    statement
You made to the *Weekly News*?' – or – 'What precisely
    is

'Your relation to Sally X – ?' A man is a bubble
Sticking to the edge of a mighty big drainpipe!

Let us be content to play one game of chess,
Share a coffee and biscuit, let Christ work out the
    deficit, –

There were eight souls, they say, with Father Noah;
Neither you nor I might have made it to the
    gangplank.


42


The rata blooms explode, the bow-legged tomcat
Follows me up the track, nipping at my ankle,

The clematis spreads her trumpet, the grassheads rattle
Ripely, drily, and all this

In fidelity to death. Today when Father Te Awhitu
Put on the black gown with the silver cross,

It was the same story. The hard rind of the ego
Won't ever crack except to the teeth of Te Whiro,

That thin man who'll eat the stars. I can't say
It pleases me. In the corner I can hear now

The high whining of a mason fly
Who carries the spiders home to his house

As refrigerated meat. 'You bugger off,' he tells me,
'Your Christianity won't put an end to death.'


46

After writing for an hour in the presbytery
I visit the church, that dark loft of God,

And make my way uphill. The grass is soaking my
    trousers,
The night dark, the rain falling out of the night,

And the old fears walk side by side with me,
Either the heavy thump of an apple

Hitting the ground, or the creaking of the trees,
Or the presence of two graveyards,

The new one at the house, the old one on the hill
That I have never entered. Heaven is light

And Hell is darkness, so the Christmen say,
But this dark is the belly of the whale

In which I, Jonah, have to make my journey
Till the fear has gone. Fear is the only enemy.

### From *How to Fly by Standing Still*

#### 3

They bring me in two eggs and a slice of bacon;
I shout and dance on the floor of the middle room

Like a chimpanzee. Joy is gripping my heart.
Their old koro has to be a madman

For them to feel at home with him. The *I Ching* tells
    me,
'Joy in movement makes people follow;

'If a man would rule he must first learn to serve' –
Thunder in the middle of the lake,

When the earth goes into winter rest
And we lie down to sleep. They honoured the men of
    old

With a tomb on the Western Mountain,
And I trust the tribes of the River will give me a tangi

Here at Jerusalem. When our bones rise again
It will be the everlasting springtime.

# C. K. STEAD

From *Twenty-one Sonnets*

*Spring 1974*

1
(1 September 1974)

Maurice, I dreamed of you last night. You wore
A black track-suit, red-striped. Saying goodbye

We fought back tears. I woke thinking you dead.
Here in the North manuka is flecked with flowers,

Willows bent in stream-beds are edged with green,
But the tall-striding poplars seem no more

Than ghostly sketches of their summer glory.
Beyond the dunes blue of the sky out-reaches

The blue of ocean where the spirits of our dead
Stream northward to their home. Under flame-trees

By Ahipara golf-course someone's transistor tells me
The news again, and down on the hard sand

In letters large enough to match the man
The children have scrawled it: BIG NORM IS DEAD.


2

Rain, and a flurry of wind shaking the pear's white
      blossom
Outside our kitchen window and tossing the lassiandra

As it did that morning four-year-old Michele Fox
Sat at our table painting shapes she said were flowers

While we listened to the news: a coaster missing up
     North,
A flare sighted in the night over Pandora Bank,

Radio contact lost – the ship's name, *Kaitawa*.
That was eight years ago. On the bus north

To Reinga and Spirits' Bay the driver remembers it –
Not a man saved, not even a body recovered,

Only smashed timber scattered down miles of coast
To tell how quickly it can come. I kept that painting –

It was the world she saw believing she had a father –
He was third engineer, a Scotsman, a good neighbour
     lost.


6

Spring hides scars on Dickens Street but the old
     cottages
Are most of them in good heart. We park outside
     number 6

My mother beside me lost in her time machine
Sixty years back when she lay behind those sashes

Staring at German ceilings, fearing a dream would end,
Her parents home after two years sailing without her.

She was seven. I know where the path ran down
Past the strawberry patch behind the red-brick
     orphanage

Whose children hung over the fence. How they must
     envy her
She thought. And when patriots chased her home from
     school

Because her name was Karlson, she didn't care too
    much.
"I'd like to die there," she says, and I feel the blessing

Of retrospect on all the griefs of Dickens Street, that
    offered
Sanctuary against the malice of the world.


9
(17 October 1974)

Spring is a recurring astonishment – like poetry.
So suddenly the oaks in Albert Park have assumed

Their bulk of green, so helplessly I find myself
With forty-two years notched up, my birthday
    presents

Hedge-clippers, screwdrivers, and *The Gulag
    Archipelago* –
And as I unwrap them a young man with a pack on his
    back

Knocks at our door wanting breakfast. His name is
    Blackburn,
Son of the 7th Fleet Admiral who rained down death

For years on North Vietnam – but the boy went to jail
Sooner than fight, and he's here to study mushrooms.

"He who forgets the past becomes blind," says
    Solzhenitsyn
In that bookful of Russian blood. "Cultivate your
    garden"

Say those Voltairean hedge-clippers. The quarrel of
    sparrows
Fills the silence of God that has lasted forty-two years.

## The Young Wife

Bees in the weatherboards
        ceilings stained with honey
the whole house is a hive.

Those mounds out there are carbodies
fencelines
        obsolete machines
dead
    and blackburied.

Since that first breathless night
I've called him Gerontion.
        If he wanted a child
why didn't he adopt me?

It's something from Wagner
        the bees are performing.
When they stop
        you hear the clicking of fleas.

Time to light the lantern.
        O eastern star

every night the same stew.


## From *Walking Westward*

Art has nothing to do with perfect circles
        squares   parallelograms
they belong to the will
even the best of moons is hand-sketched
        effulgence-blurred
but a rough triangle
        that's different
the Nile Delta for example
or what Antony saw first and last in Cleopatra

a blunt arrow-head of crisp hair
                    pointing the way
down
        into another dimension
only perfect world
                    slippery sided
inward-enclosing
                welcome
and welcome
                and welcome
"die when thou hast lived"
and all the perfumes of Arabia couldn't rival what the
        lady made there
who called him infirm of purpose
talked of plucking a baby's toothless gums from her
        breast
and dashing its brains out
because he could not use a dagger
would not draw a circle about her brows.


October she phoned to say
for her at last it was   over
                        forgotten
                        irrelevant
3 nails meant for the heart

might have made use of the new maths
that has a cold beauty
like the beauty of a fiction

as for example that a survey of 19 love affairs showed
            17 were over
            7 were forgotten
            and 13 irrelevant
            but only 2 were all three
9 were over and irrelevant but not forgotten
5 were over and forgotten but not irrelevant
how many that were over were neither irrelevant nor
        forgotten?

to which a Venn diagram
viz:

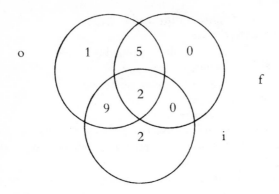

returns the answer 1
(rendered poetically: one only)
                    irrefutable
as to say in the language of another dimension
he had explored with her
the caves of generation and the terraces of the stars


*This may be your captain speaking*

Moon moon moon moon this
obsession darkness and clear
light over water the beach
Takapuna winds from all quarters

on vacation small waves
lifting with that breath–
catching moon–reflecting
pause its flash or shimmer

running down their raised
foil before falling the whole
Gulf across to Rangitoto
listening and over it a

huge havenless heaven alight
all the way out to the end
of the ever. But it's the sea's
particular talk these words

spaced out between wave-
break in every of its modes one
beach having one voice settlers
heard ancient Maoris came

upon a characterizing
untranslatable statement under
pohutukawas endlessly
varied endlessly the same.

# VINCENT O'SULLIVAN

## Talking to Her

Talking to her is stepping from a street,
from traffic and sun and the racket of news
to a hospital lobby, where feet
click on lino, where the jaunty lose

the springiness of their walk, are told
Wait here until the Authorities are free.
Or Come in, you can visit now, old
and young and sick are all there to see.

I imagine a ward with row upon row
of patients, some sleeping, a few
sighing to themselves, a dream of snow
over beds sedation is flooding through.

And there are other doors for the dying
and a room with bars across the pane.
The smell of the air scours deceit and lying.
I have never been anywhere so sane.

## Bus Stop

A cat walks on the barracks roof.
From here, in this light,
pale fawn spots on its murky belly,
it could be a thing left over
from firing practice, nicks of sky
seen through it.
                    Later, it comes to the tables,
its flecked eyes indifferent to your own,
no sign of pleasure should you drop it
a scrap of bone, none of offence
that you stare back at it, ignore
its soft, lean, alert scrounging

between chair and chair.

Not much to remember a place by,
a spatter-coloured cat
to make one think months after
of army, of food,
            of something less than people
which is also hungry.
As close as one brushes with truth
                in half an hour.


### From *Brother Jonathan, Brother Kafka*

8

On the day my father died a flame-tree
with its stiff immaculate flares cupped over
the leafless branches outside the hospital window
said for us several things voice could not get round to,

yet not only and not foremost the riding of life
above the stark branches nor the perfect *Fin*
once the work is done, as though time's shining
is when the match is struck and is over, so.

It spoke, each opening red fist only feet from dying,
of small errors, of mornings forgotten by afternoon,
of words taken or words put down lightly
as a glass, or laid like a single log on a fire,

or touched as the head of a child absently
while other words moved on; the looks,
brushings, immediate treasure, the cusps of morning
lifting as sky lightens the withholding tree.

## 9

This talking of death in itself is *getting over:*
is raising a curtain in the morning for a minute
above that blunt freshness, and looking at the yard,
the four green plastic buckets, the Y.M.C.A.

three blocks away easing smoke
from its high chimney at a blue sky
                              – spring sky because acacia
as thinnish, wiry, as trees manage, carries

a rubbed blur against it, the hint of leaves,
and you take them in – the smoke, the tree
above the buckets, the curtain bunched up
in your left hand, before you remember,

before it's her hair you see teeming against a chair
or a voice you'll not hear again and have almost heard
or the shine along a coffin you thought you'd never
    forget.
But the curtain still in your hand, you know that you
    do.

## 13

To be in a place for spring and not have lived its winter
is to get things on the cheap – it is asking from sky   *beyond*
as much as taking from earth, what has not been   *earthly thing*
    earned,
it is food without its growing, pay without labour,

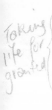

*Taking life for granted*

love and not its unpredictable effort
at kindness, tact – in fact, it is how we live.   *Trying to make this*
I sit in a room where each day the heaters   *as easy as poss*
burn for an hour less; I see trees

which I saw neither in leaf nor when their leaves

were called for, prepare for spring,
                              I am like a man
arriving too late for Friday's riddled flesh
or Saturday's dreadful inertia, and then on Sunday
          hearing

a corpse walks on the hillside, shining and placid,
asks 'What's so special?'
                          A man in spring
without winter or the fear which is properly winter's
is Thomas's gullible brother,
                        so much sillier than doubt.

15

I begin to get like a guy in the movies – I eat
Reizenstein bread and blueberry cakes and drink coffee
it seems at any hour while I sit at a counter
and stir the coffee with a kind of spatula.

Between my times at the counter I more or less work
as a cow digests between turns in the stalls.
I read a man of God who tied excellence and pleasure
to the mere act of perceiving, made the instant of sense

the moment of will, and thus is man defined –
meaning hell or heaven by how you take things in.
The recipe is near perfect.
                        It puts shits where you want them
and the good a little closer to real service.

It makes mood and tantrum the ugly meat they are
and a clean disposition like a starched napkin
you finger through grace.
                          'So what'll it be, buster?'
is one kind of asking.
          '*Name* it for me, Brother Edwards,' is another.

31

Everyman true to himself as Whitman – and that goes
for the whole caboodle, the guard on the train who says
'Happy July 4th', or the crowd crammed above the
    Hudson
to see two centuries sail in, the tall ships hoisting


the dream high again, high as the statue's
torch or some remote governor's steeple-
crowned hat, God at home *again* on his faithful heads,
in his New Canaan – or the strutting pimp corner

of 8th Ave and 44th whose buckles wink
in the sun, whose heels lift him from mere earth,
asks with his hip gangling shuffle
'Bicentennial fuck, sah?' – and his head flickers

like his tongue to the wigged doorways, the cottonfields
of Aquarius –
                    as Whitman then, saying 'I find
no sweeter fat than sticks to my bones,' the lesson
to end them all.
                    The first people who sang it, sing it, sing.


32

A young bee falls between my window
and the wire screen. It slips as it climbs at one,
is caught with legs and rough belly against the mesh
of the other. I raise the screen slightly and it shoots


across to sunlight, a small furred bullet.
So another, five years ago, I remember, catching
beneath an infant's singlet and stinging his chest.
The child clutched his breath, looked it seemed with
    appalling

wisdom at those who fussed about him, who
rubbed ointment on the red welt, carried
the bee to the porch in a scrap of paper
and stamped it on the boards.
                    The boy looked and moved

his head to take in the kitchen, the relations,
the afternoon of his first summer, the pain rising
on his body while he still forbore crying . . .
                    On, on through endless summers,
the look of the boy looking, the bee never crushed.


## 33

My landlady has been to Hawaii. I look at her diamante
glasses, her dyed hair, her fifty-four as she confesses
years but I guess sixty at a pinch. Christ, one thinks,
she's going to tell it all! 'Say, did I mention this?'

she begins. She starts to strip me to my affected bones.
Her talk is as pure as the bay Cook must have come to
with Venus in mind. She speaks of the natives with awe,
she makes the flowers live and open for you as she

tells you, the long axes of the surf, the broken volcanic
pillars behind the Holiday Inns and the Hiltons,
the valley she went to by bus and distinguishes as a child
might with its frankness – 'It's like where we'd all

want to be born, want our own to be born' –
she tells it while her glasses wink and I feel ashamed
that until now I remembered only a place I brooded
at the edge of the same sea, bored where Eden ends.


## 35

A day bloated with statistics. A quarter of the States

will be struck by 'flu by the Fall – a similar strain
to the one which accounted for twenty million
in 1918. At the theatre in College Street

there is a Jewish concert on the 26th in memory
of the six million. A visiting speaker
says each word of Solzhenitsyn is a drop
from the veins of – how many myriads is it?

The human animal's not geared to carry
such choke of numbers. There's the swelling under
    your left
rib, maybe, the fear you have at the sharp contraction
as you wake in the night; there's remembering to ask
    your grocer

about Loreta his daughter who was taken in on Sunday
with savage pains in her head. There's the drunken
    old bitch
in the bar who cadges. There's an epileptic keeps claiming
she slipped.
    None of us, none, can lug so very much more.


## 44

*Between the two follies I return and return to –*
*the Puritan razor paring towards bone's*
*perfection, Edwards' exquisitely-wired machine*
*for grace, destruction – between this and Kafka's*

*delicious and simple gloom, man to the last minute*
*refuting the point of the unopened door, the executioner's*
*tact, the ant's absurd wholeness beneath*
*the falling rock,* between: *the dancing place,*

*the breath's ritzy colosseum, the full flutter*
*of flag and flag along the skyline, the foreshore,*
*the whirred diamonds salty in delighted eyes*

*where a child kicks at the ocean's withers,*

*where he canters creating himself a stallion*
*whose hooves lace in the slanted lapsing*
*between wave and wave, beast whose back is a prairie*
*and the child himself standing, irreducible grain.*

## Late Lunch, San Antonio

We sit and talk over lunch of the inevitable blow-out,
agree with the savants of TV shows, the scientists

whose theoretical clock now stands so close to 12,
share the hysteria as before football matches

when the girls prance their pom-poms and the mascot
runs round the sideline dragging the other team's
        colours.

The airs in San Antonio in March
stretch so high, so purely blue, a hawk or likewise a
        dove

could be picked up you'd think at countless thousand
        feet.
A man says "When it's too late . . .",

when the hardware's on due course and set target
and there's no going back on that one any more

than you stand up parthenons or observatories or
        suburban houses
once the principle that holds them has clapped out;

in that "state of wargasm" as he calls it
it's as if we'll be in a tent of pure illumination.

*Tabernaculum* will take on a new drift, *shekinah*

perk up as it hasn't for a milennium or two.

We'll have done it at last, be the power we've always
    cringed at.
In the glare of such election, slap backs, call each other
    Moses.


## Further Instructions

"Go down to the zoo," Rodin told Rilke. "Go and take
    a look."
At the sow reality, one presumes. At the baboon's

delectably outrageous arse, the swift furl,
unfurl, of all that elephant's spongey trunk,

the ibis spearing at fish neatly as a nib.
Go down to the zoo where the adjectives and such

are jungle & swamp & bush and the animals
appear above, through, over, in spite of.

Take a look. Let your eye cast its own bronze,
the bronze of pure occasion justify your eye.

# MICHAEL JACKSON

## Sudan

Region of our disdain,
whose quiet men have injury
and pillaged caravans in their gaze;
I came here
to obtain no silver, no provisions
for my journey back,
but to look into the eyes
of men who no longer own the earth
of women who abandon the black tents
at dusk
and descend
to draw water for any stranger.

## The Red Flag

A night of iron wheels and rain,
the judder and crash of wagons
coupling each valley to a metal road
and the nasal shriek of the train's
severing echo half way from home
to nowhere, I listen to you play
*The Red Flag* on your harmonica,
railroaded into cinder yards
on the abrupt last day of childhood.

1931. Your father just come back
from three months jail; you stand
among his comrades in a smoke-filled
railway waiting room; the train
blacks out the lamps; they take him
away. A child then, four years
old, accomplice to events
you do not understand, and your mother
won't or can't explain.

For the need of heroes in a hard time
the orphaning of those who wake
to the night train whistle in the hills,
play *Tannenbaum*, pine tree, wind, cones
and branches on an iron roof. In
Marion street you wait for your girl
while west of Himatangi the barrow
of an old embankment covered with lupins
covers your father's tracks.

### Australia

All the blues in the world
are here. This is the continent
where blue is quarried.

Along the tracks
where blue was traded
where cobalt and perse were casked and packed
blue has been spilled;
the hills are steeped in it
it has been ambushed in the night
it has settled on the leaves like smalt
it has been carried away by rivers
it has been washed into the livid sea
it has drifted into the sky.

Beryl, turquoise, opal, indigo,
the blue in the bone cages of eucalypts
on the bluffs near Eden;
the moths in the saxe-blue dusk at Tidbinbilla;
Nowa Nowa, Cann River,
where the measure of distance is always blue.

And where the blue goes when it dies?

Into the desert, where there is nothing
but spirits, penumbral, of the colour blue.

## Neanderthal

Who never knew to sow
seeds on the floodplain every year,
harvest, store, dig metals
from the earth for war

Buried their children
and those whom age had harmed
with care

Placed at the feet a graven
stone, at the head
food offerings, around
the body
wild cornflowers, mallow,
milfoil, lilac
and rare herbs.

Do not imagine them
with brutish hands,
crag-browed, unkempt, ill-
spoken, who nursed and minded
these unlucky ones:

An arthritic one-armed
cripple at Shanidar,
a ten year old boy at Namur;
their children
who numbered half the deaths
by cold and hunger,
disease or accident,
are buried here.

## Mask-maker

For years we endured his insolence
as he worked on, carving

in the avoided wood
faces we could not see.

At festival or market
set by the stars, a grim display:
how he became us and mocked our chief,
found out bad parentage, illicit
love, confronted our intent
with consequence.

To me he gave this mask
smudged with charcoal and red clay,
to my neighbour this
abandoned hearth,
and to another madness, smoke and ash,
and to us all the curse of secrecy.

# ALAN LONEY

## Of flowers

'by jesus christ' he said
'look at that, we're living
in paradise an we don't know it
lilies, an, an gerANiums, beautiful
BEAUTiful,   we're living
in bloody PARAdise,
                              haha
                                   you know
this crook leg's getting better, no
really, i could walk a hundred bloody miles. . .

it's funny when ya think about it
but no matter what ya do
in this life ya have
ta pay, right down
to the
          uttermost
                         farthing
     by jesus
     flowers are
     bloody
     wonderful
                    haha

remind ya of women, don't they'


## Elegy     1

youd make capital of

my destiny & death, smasht & jointed,
the split carriage
          water soup'd by our blood,
my left arm vomited on by those

who cdnt stand the sight?

You cdnt bear it
    more than I / less than I,
oblivious of
    the yellow light hanging
        thru what trees passd, that hold hills
           freshen air by stream

        & the Catholic school, Peter, Paul
     & the love of Cain

till awakend by wood
    & metal, screeching & awry beneath me
      soft on Mother's breast

her care & pain a man had pusht
    off. Us off.
Hail Marys be damnd
    & me just 10, & snuffd.     Grains of
dirt

strewn thru my body

### *The eternal return*

bury the corngod. Throw yr shovel
up, to the highest ear yet.
               Drag that sun
from its oceanbed, pick the 1st
flower, lever again these islands
into the light.

Let Spring take on, so. For gods'
for a child's sake let Spring take on. Open
yr mouth wide for snow. There's

a return takes you back, & green

is symptom of. Back to original
dawn & origins/the 1st fact/delineation of
tracks from here to Hell, to
Heaven/the names of

all denizens.    Atoms & meteors on
the milkman's round, we also learnt, then, & now.

Bury nothing


## Elegy    2

the 'crusher' never scared me. Tho that giant
   of a man had his foot cut
      clean, downwards, thru his boot
his heel intact

Bones & shingle, ground
   in the riverdredge.

Even at night, the place
   like Usher, was friendly
      compared to the cemetery
       across from it,
weeds chest-high, names
   obliterate, wroughtiron that cdnt hold
      back the feel of air
       about bones,
& grass rattling along the fence –

*then* I'd run
        / past the timberyard,
out-of-bounds, the house of
   the Indian girl who opend
      my 1st open approach,

& on home, to listen to 'Christ boy
        you go thru sandals!

                              Waddya *do* with them?'

        ((& why *he* shambled around
          trailing my mother
          I dont know

                    *Elegy*   6

in my collection, the words are, we use
        & have use of us,

edged by, no hope, but traps
        that'd take yr foot off

The sweet lips of learning.
The arse of speech.
All holes interchangeable
        at my age, boy, so like yr father
                I calld you 'son' getting off the bus

So, 'beach' I like. Shell bits trodden
        into the asphalt, a shingle easy
                for their young bare feet
                        to run on,
                                but not 'sea'. Not any sort of
terror like that. Its white tongue
        pewking into yr throat – no-one needs that
                sort of garbage.
                                Do you know,
the bastard once calld me a shrew.   'View'
        is another I like. Another bludgeon
                to lessen force. Newfangled camera. My dream
                        real.   o, lovely in white, &

act out, nothing.   I seem only to grip
        the early things.

That poor stutterer will disappoint
        who gave him birth

# RACHEL McALPINE

### *the test*

I have arranged a final test
and a white sky leaking

arranged for a tree outside to shake
and shake and shake its pretty white hats

set up an iron bed   (it's bed you want)
with a bottle and tube some bleeding and some blood

I invite you in to meet me
in my elderly yellow face

I dare you to come close come here
has the tree defeated you?

dying is a blurring and a slow retreat
a bleaching of the blue and brown of you

I grope at you for signs of your dissolving
o my sweet my sweet


### *three poems for your eyes*

i

your eyes are in khaki
are you at war
or on safari?

I would hate to be a pet
but I am scared of dying


ii

you have cat's eyes and they glow

in the daytime flashing
go and go and go

come to me and I'll melt
the glass turn off the light
and lie on pussy willow


iii


the way the grey-green water
settles into the hollow and
swivels in its socket

the way the green diminishes
and grey thickens and winces
as the wind crams the clouds
across the bay

and how your eyes flick and
heal so quickly after
the harbour darkens above me


*on the train*

a woman may talk to a woman
and a man may talk to a man

the lady tells of how her husband
died and how she has this headache

all the time but pills
make her fat or fall over

she has settled for a head
full of sausage meat

does she think of dying

and of after dying?

sometimes she does and last week
she bought a cocktail cabinet

she knows the secret of the anaesthetic
how it pulls you to the black space

where God is not and truth blows fiercely
(o how to hold on to the lies!)

the nurses hold her hand
watching her cry

watching without surprise
her soul clambering back

people are good to her

# DAVID MITCHELL

### *windfall*

th oranges in th bowl
really belong
to ward 7.

th nurse / however / has
brought them in here
'fr th children'

they don't amount to much
small, bruised fruit, still
there they are
       on th window sill. . .
familiar suns
against th willow pattern
dark blue & ice
& th 'sensuous rill' ah!
some kind of paradise.

th oranges in th bowl
are / undeniably / larger
than life
      to maureen fiona
              chantal. . .
yeah.
well, she's 4 / nearly 5
still
glad to be alive / &

lucky.

    1 broken arm
    3 broken ribs
    fractured skull
    & massive shock. . . yeah. &
she

has lain there   2 weeks
beneath this world's crass clock
in th bruised pits of 'reality'
feeling / 'a bit cold'
watching th dust motes dance
in th early sun (as of old)
& considering th gold cheeks
of th oranges . . .
she's lying there / alone / discreetly
watching th sun make time
with its own (as of old) & sweetly!
&
sweetly.

tomorrow th aliens come
th woman & th man
tomorrow is th birthday
(she's forgotten th other, darker anniversary)
tomorrow there will be gifts in th nursery
- - - according to th plan; yeah. looks
'of love' / & story books / with th pictures above
a doll
    an apple / maybe / & a ginger
    bread man . . . yeah. & voices; voices; voices
    from some star . . .
    (she's forgotten whose they are)

potato chips? licorice, darling?
    a
      mars
          bar?


        *celebrant*

this slender girl
sprawled on th buffalo grass
dreams
    of some dark prince

from out another life


& of horses, too
& of horses.


th afternoon quickens with rain
high
above th sullen grey / there
is borne
th silver sound
of a long, jet, aeroplane . . .


she's 22
          / already broken
on th blue wheel of love
(& that's some rub)
& she
does not know or care
what machinery round her moves
th spectral spokes or rim
& she
is delving in
to self
          & fretting at th hub


aware/
      only
of wild horses moving through
th dream
& th dove


diminishing along th broken
air . . .

this girl
sprawls on th grass
& beneath her th earth moves
& above, some machine
& beyond that, th sun &
some
  kind
    of melody . . .


above her / life moves
but she
is sunk beneath
    quite another rhythm
    & hears

    only hooves

only hooves.

# ELIZABETH SMITHER

## Song about my father

My father when the sulphur boats were in
Wore sulphur in his eyebrows
Like a Galapagos finch

My mother spread a gingham cloth
Cleaned cupboards, baked on Tuesdays
Kept her children's hair brushed

He was a sort of bee.
The gleaming thorax of the two-stroke
James shattered the air above the asphalt

His eyebrows I recall like vines
Hid the eyes of a nightbird
Customed to the splash of the sea

He always returned when the moon
Took over its watch
Leaving the sleeping scaffolding in the port.


## Sugar Daddy

Crouched by the casino like a white rabbit
You wait with your cold silver watch.
The night smells of furs and taxis
Cachous and wet puddles. Persian lamb
Glove turns up Persian lamb collar, the
French almonds slide in the lining
Of your heart. Poor rabbit, like a corsage
Of dried everlasting flowers, stocks and shares
Green and purple in the fluorescence.
Here she glides your not-too-close dream

Bosomed like twin gloves in Drake's
Dark study, turning to your death
Like an undiscovered new world.


## The beak

He's a little man with a corporation who can say
Private parts as though it's butterfly cakes.
His mouth opens like a scissors and white air
Pours through smelling of ether. He's known for years
And years that words are the killer.
He chooses his carefully then betrays the jury
(Your accumulated experience) to decide.
Some days he calls the tea break early.
We rise to 'Stand for his Honour, the Queen's Judge'.
But he quickly asks us to sit, he dislikes
Honour and such words. Pressing his pale
Parchment fingertips together he says
You, the jury, will look for corroboration, believe no
    one.
At lunch under escort in a nearby restaurant
Where the police escorts amusingly eat through the
    menu
We see him pass in a black homburg, not eating
Himself, or speaking, just taking the air.


## The Feast of All Saints

The napery in heaven's wind
Dries and is set down
With candles and unearthly flowers.
Twelve places at each table:
The saints in perfect agape.

Grace can last for hours
And be in a minute over
They break the bread in slow motion
The wine freezes in a stream.
Laughter chants around their heads.

He is not coming. It is theirs alone
Like a dorm party at midnight
They clown their roles but cannot spoil their robes.
Whatever they fought with on earth
Is removed now: they fight like doves.


### Change of School

Sister Veronica's class. A tall nun with a pale
Greer Garson face who embraces him in the doorway
Gives him her linen kiss and wraps her arms
(Bat wings) like a door. Safe in the clutch
Of the church he beams and I go off happy.
By noon he recites how they whoop and jump
On their desks when sister's out of the room,
Then subside when she comes in gliding.
Already she has penetrated like convent walls
The secret wraith passages of his brain
Glides there in his first garden, a patch
Of cleared ground the size of a saucer
Where he grows his one geranium of love.

Three days later he is transferred to another class.


*Fr Anselm Williams and Br Leander Neville hanged by Lutheran
mercenaries in 1636 while out of their monastery on a local errand of
charity — from the guidebook to Ampleforth Abbey and College.*

'We'll see who can stick
Their tongue out first for God

Out of you two,' binding the hands
The flowers in the hedgerows starting
The sky turning over with a lurch
As when Brother Leander dropped the eggs.
They wouldn't be back to Compline
The hedgeroses looked askance now.
A swallow passed. Their hands touched
Just the fingertips like passing a note.
The tongues would come out later
Into an air gone blue, a world.

# SAM HUNT

*Notes from a Journey*
*(for Hone)*

When I left Wanganui
(you and Eve asleep still
low under canvas) my pilgrimage
was northward up
the river of the three taniwha

The sun shone; every little
township had its one-way bridge.
By midday, man, it seemed
a month instead of
half a day since leaving

Three o'clock that afternoon
I picked up three local boys,
Tawe, Gabriel, Andrew;
drove them through
Pipiriki out to Raetihi

They told me of Hemi, how
a month ago he walked
the whole way out on foot
'27 bloody miles of it!'
He died soon after that

'What if we meet old Hemi
around the next bend?' I asked.
'Let the bugger walk it'
one boy laughed. I turned
laughing with him

His face was dust and tears.
I passed him the bottle,
double declutching,
chopping down the gears.
It was a steep, slow climb.

### Stabat Mater

My mother called my father 'Mr Hunt'
For the first few years of married life.
I learned this from a book she had inscribed:
'To dear Mr Hunt, from his loving wife.'

She was embarrassed when I asked her why
But later on explained how hard it had been
To call him any other name at first, when he –
Her father's elder – made her seem so small.

Now in a different way, still like a girl,
She calls my father every other sort of name;
And guiding him as he roams old age
Sometimes turns to me as if it were a game . . .

That once I stand up straight, I too must learn
To walk away and know there's no return.

### April Fool

*It's the old tricks is best tricks*
*cause only the best tricks survive*

So,
up behind our hill
behind the macrocarpa belt
this God-almighty glow.

A fire first I thought how will
the engine ever get up there?

I changed my mind I thought those
new neighbours they're
always having parties.
Not like at our place.

I clambered up, wanting most I guess
a rock-and-roll band whacking
shit from up the hill. Floodlights,
everything I thought the whole
damn lot.

Instead, full on and lifting
out of heavy cloud,
the moon. Up to her old
tricks I thought.

# BILL MANHIRE

### *The elaboration*

there was a way out of here:
it went off in the night
licking its lips

the door flaps like a great wing:
I make fists at the air
and long to weaken

ah, to visit you
is the plain thing,
and I shall not come to it

### *The poetry reading*

The green fields. The green fields.
How beautiful they are.
How beautiful they are.

This next poem is about the green fields
Which are to be found in England.
They contain certain small animals
Which have chosen to make their life there.

The public has constant access to them.
Not to the animals, as you might
Understandably think, but to the green fields
In which they have chosen to make their homes.

### *The collection*

1

All day at the lake we watched

cars, the red guts of mountains.
You lay back at the edge of
water & demonstrated my lack
of perfection: the trick of
the bird, sliding down a rainbow.

Later you bring on all your
effects: & in the garden we discover
the skating-rink, women ticking
with white frost, as if they
mean to go off. A farmer from
Balclutha sends a platoon of sheep

out on to the ice. In their little
boots they are quite graceful.
They surround three women &
shepherd them in for inspection.
You sail out from me, shaking
ice from your shoulders.

2

The room goes back about
one month's journeying,
past a pet cat & a few musicians,
to where a number of people
are celebrating Christmas.

My father is dreaming of
a white mistress. That is
his joke, he is utterly
deluded, but you fit the bill.

My mother is looking for
the arrival of Christ. She needs
only a small opportunity,
only no one will provide it.

In the garden, flowers
thicken with each kiss.
My friends, never in danger,
make a perfect descent from
the tree. The moon drives
light into your spine.

We are all here, with
a smattering of language.
It seems we have gone
overboard for sincerity.


3


Well,

you have become my favourite
neighbour, merely by being
in the right place at the
right time. In mid-flight
on the swing in your garden,
clutching a bucket of clothes-
pegs, hovering over the carrots,
you are my very best friend.

Your journeys are crowded with
little forks: some are mine,
& a few you have on approval.
On New Year's Eve we take up
the collection. You retreat
into the hedge & reach out
your fingers, as if you mean
something by it. Like

the magician's magic hand
depositing the ace of spades
in a lady's knickers.
The music. The music of water.

## Summer

### 1

It is so white.

It divides under the snow.
It wakes alone, a sensational pleasure.

### 2

Supposing this page is a paddock
under snow, or rather supposing
this page is snow

blanketing the paddock
then these lines

must be tracks in the whiteness
left by animals late at night.

Or fences, or trees
just risking the surface.

### 3

Possibly the bodies of lovers are also present,
though almost invisible to the naked eye.

### 4

See?

And occasionally, one supposes,
some marriage may be celebrated.

5

Or, this word may be a boulder,
or this, or this

or this, which is a stone,
on which the poet sits, somewhat alone,
saying, 'Hell, another masterpiece.'


*The importance of personal relationships*

Let's just reject
discussion, the safety of
numbers

and go to
sleep in a
serious fashion. Dancing

on God's
veiny wrist, for instance, leaping
the veins: I mean, we

could manage that more
often. *How do
you do how*

*do you
do?* I am fine thank
you.


*Wulf*

1

They take it from me:
in the manner

of a gift

*if danger moves in the earth*
*is the life given*
*is it love between us*


2


*Wulf:* on that island
        *— I on this other*

shut into fens, a bone
in the neck of a savage

*if danger moves upon water*
*is the life given*
*is it love between us*


3


In my mind we joined together:

as it rained, as
I was sad in the rain, as
he laid me with his arms

into his shoulder
a joy given into me like sorrow


4


*Wulf, Wulf,*
            it is not
at all hunger shaking my limbs
but that you do not journey

absent & yet
you fill me


### 5

They take it from me:
            in the manner
of a gift

*the spine of a feather, a cloud in the body*

            ai, it is
easily broken, what

was never at one:

you & I, *Wulf*, the one
with the other

& singing


### Wellington

It's a large town
full of distant figures on the street
with occasional participation.
Someone buys some shares,
another gets a piece of the action.
Foreign languages are spoken.
A good secretary
is worth her weight in gold.
The man himself
is sitting on a little goldmine.
And down on Lambton Quay
the lads in cars go past, it's raining,
and the boys from Muldoon Real Estate
are breaking someone's arm.

They don't mean harm, really, it's
nobody's business, mainly free
instructive entertainment,
especially if you don't get close
but keep well back like
all the distant figures in the crowd.
So you watch what you can
but pretend to inspect with interest instead
the photographs of desirable private
properties, wondering how close they go
to government valuation. That one's nice.
The question is, do you put your hands
above your head or keep them
in your pockets. Do you want a place
without a garage, could you manage
all those steps. The answer is
the man would simply like you off the streets.
You haven't even got a window
and his is full of houses.


### Party Going

It's lonely in the world
when all you get is pity.
The grass is tall and straight
and sometimes waving in the wind.
It grows around the sleeping lovers
and though the police are coming
they somehow look remoter. The last time
I saw you, you said you really
wanted to go home but you had this feeling
you were being followed. You were
half in darkness, half in light,
going outside with all the others.

## *Last things*

The kids want to grow up
and be on the phone and everything.
When they throw stones into the creek
they want to make a decent splash,
they want to get that stranglehold
on water. As usual words of praise
conclude the story we were just
beginning to read
but flipped to the end instead:
the family dog was strong and safe
and underneath himself, no one
was lonely. The stone like stone
hit bottom and was obsolete.

# IAN WEDDE

*Losing the Straight Way*

1

I lie down & take off my body/
I lie down letting my head drop sideways
losing my way.
Somehow at the centre of my life
& the seasons come into me

caresses  waking into dreams.

Getting back into
ordinary summer/streets
grown fuller with the green
trees someone planted, left behind.

Giuliana, this miracle:
waking to dawn & birds
flocking past the bright window
like those fragments of messages
which flew off into other poems,
which return now to their season/

& no revelations, but
women  known secrets in whose hair
sun spins like morning in the spokes
of a child's bicycle through the park
against that new green.

Men & women step
into each other fling open the shutters &
air their place.
Thus it all comes round
again, light green & love,
& now blossom & shattered sunlight
among the buildings:

these very rich hours

for which almost everything must change/

jade lodes press up
& veins to the surface

sweet sap rising through
280 days.
It sounds like more than a season.

At its close
pale streets
drawn back upon their bones/

This, Giuliana Mieli:
which I want you to be among the first to know,

who sleeps in that part of me
which I think resembles *una selva oscura*

a wood dark with growth.

So you may be among the first to bless us.


2


That autumn day suddenly broken into
by pale sunlight          a hearse
glittered darkly across the intersection
between two buildings
which seemed to lean aside
as light drove between them.
& lately: atavistic dreams: flying/
water/ swimming against the stream.
If I compound these images
I compound too much since
I know how we like to make dialogues thus

& thus, her voice floating
from her mouth, the bed full of
blood, the second heart silent,
the wave suspended, the
wave falling, the moment before
we cry out, our fires
licking into each other. I know
how we like to imagine this hiatus
endures like the process
it's only part of. Why
then does some vestigial part of me press &
press to believe
there's a price for everything.


3


I imagine the womb as a honeycomb

I imagine the womb as a kind of lung
& the child within breathed into

'part & not part' / stirring as if with
breath in the roseate glow of daylight
strained through blood

I imagine the womb as an early morning
in autumn        filled
with the weary movements of trees

I imagine the womb as a city
where you might meet a friend or enemy
& be unable to embrace him or
make your peace with him because the crowds
moved on & moved on

I imagine the womb as a universe
& the child as an asteroid
travelling so swiftly it is motionless

across distances so vast it stops forever

I imagine the womb as a gourd
rattling against the house wall

I imagine the womb as a pod
which must rupture to ease the hungers of mankind

I imagine the womb as a kind of deep river pool
in which the river's currents become invisible
unless the eye can detect a dead gnat moving down the
    surface

unless the palate can taste the timeless alluvia
of what sustains us

I imagine the womb as the blank centre of a girl's eye
which the world

penetrates with its images

I imagine the womb as a honeycomb

as a lung

as an autumn morning

as a moving city

as a universe

as a dry gourd

as a bursting pod

as a pool

as the pupil of an eye

### 4

Their mouths crept together for comfort.

Their lips crept together for silence.

The mouths of their wounds
crept together for concealment.

Beneath white lips of scars
their blood      ran on in silence.


## From *Earthly: Sonnets for Carlos*

### 2

*it's time*

A beautiful evening, early summer.
I'm walking from the hospital. His head
was a bright nebula
                    a firmament
swimming in the vulva's lens . . . *the colour
of stars/* "Terraces the colour of stars . . ."

I gazed through my tears.
                         The gifts of the dead
crown the heads of the newborn            She said
"It's time" & now I have a son            time for

naming the given
                the camellia
which is casting this hoar of petals (stars?)
on the grass . . . all winter the wind kept from
the south, driving eyes & heart to shelter.
Then came morning when she said "It's time, it's
time!"      time's
                careless nebula of blossom/

*2 for Rose*

9

"If thy wife is small bend down to her &
whisper in her ear" (Talmud)

                         – what shall I
whisper?     that I dream it's no use any
more trying to hide my follies. If trees &

suchlike don't tell on me I understand
my son will & soon, too. His new blue eyes
see everything. Soon he'll learn to see
less. O the whole great foundation is sand.

But the drought has broken today, this rain!
pecks neat holes in the world's salty fabu-
lous diamond-backed carapace & doubt comes
out, a swampy stink of old terrapin.

What shall I say? "I hid nothing from you,
but from myself. That I dream, little one,

10

by day & also by night & you are
always in the dream . . ." Oh you can get no
peace, will get none from me. The flower smells so
sweet who needs the beans? We should move house
    there
into the middle of the bean-patch: a
green & fragrant mansion, why not! Let's do
it all this summer & eat next year. O

let's tear off a piece. It's too hard & far
to any other dreamt-of paradise
& paradise is earthly anyway,
earthly & difficult & full of doubt.

I'm not good I'm not peaceful I'm not wise
but I love you. What more is there to say.
My fumbling voices clap their hands & shout.


53

*hello*

"Hello"      his first word
                            "Hallo" or "Halloa"
"Halloo"
            *Do not halloo until you're out*
of the wood
                  oscura
                        ché la dirita
via era . . .
            *halgian?* to hallow
*halowen?* holler, howl.
                            or just "Hello"
meaning "I recognize you oh please don't
lower your eyes"   •          my fumbling voices
      shout

out Hello!
            (halloa!) camellia
firmament   (halloo!) diamond carapace

Howling in the dark wood and hallowing
the ways out of it
                  you here among them
among the unruly facts & fragments
we recognise again, hello'ing
them & howling them & hallowing them

### Cardrona Valley

'Grown men'
                those kids pissing into a clay bank.
All for love of that preterite
beaten thin as air by the centuries.

The badeyed steer stales like a busted conduit.
The river gobbles rocks.
The commonage didn't last either.

After rain the mushrooms come snouting up
each one the hardon of a buried miner
dreaming what his dirt will buy.

Mouth of dark spaces
the valley waits for the mountain.

### Beautiful Poultry

Slipped it under a mothering
hen while she slept, thought
she might not turn it out
& next morning

her brood was larger by one
which one, 'my one', who knew:
survival's anonymous
& ungrateful & we need

more than that, we need
Beauty, Mandelstam's
'plain carpenter's fierce rule of eye',
intuitive alignments with the Infinite, oh

boy! we say, this egg's
so beautiful! & we gild it, it's
exquisite. It has
a dead chicken inside.

### Dark Wood

1

The phrase goes on growing in my head
a tree fixing its roots in me:

> 'in the middle of
> the journey of     *our* life'
> articulated

logging trucks hit low gear
down the main road.
                masts of those hills
riding at anchor on their strata, compactions
                of generations: the food
of the living

                whose tissues I hear
tearing before the
bright saw.     the masthead
tipping, the earth-sea
shaking at the fall:

                a swath
mown through the fleet: a thousand
of them skilfully
                'taken out': a tithe

of what I think is beautiful
a commingling of elements
though another forest once grew there/

                but *this* usurping
                dark wood
where no birds live, where the foot-
fall's also silent in the
sour detritus, siftings
upon siftings

& a sea smell, piercing,

cloacal.       where fungi
grow like rotten coral from the sea-bed/

                    but this
                    dark wood

's a seeming, a symbol, whose
mystery.
                    whose mastery
I enter        whose masts      whose airy
corruptions I enter & am lost in


                    2


                    : as a man might be lost
in that space where the battered hull's
held tenderly against the wharf–buffers
where the same deep redolence rises
                    where the same light sifts

                    & the logs
swing over.       the iron tackle
clangs, the chains are loosed.
The logs drop to their allotted place.
They will cross the Ocean of
Conrad's dark heart.
They will be whittled into matchsticks

                    & sent back.       little
masts       mysteries. to light
                    your fire.


                    3

If you know anything

you line the grain up & strike to the side.

I get short ends from the wharf
for winter. I saw them up.
Then I split them & stack them.
The bright blade
breaks the grain     the timber cracks     I
breathe its sea-gasp.
Stacked, a spring tide.     the dark shed
sails in a reek of pitch

          airy fragrance
of destruction.     the wood
burns bright & quick. the
          ash goes
back to earth     the gas
          to air.     A handful
a breath
of what the tree fed on.

4

          If you know
anything.     *in*
-*spiration*: whatever comes out at last
& must be purified

          again.     I split Language
          to make poems burn.     to have
          beauty usurp
          beauty.     comminglings of elements.
the broken ends of tithes of airy masts
split/ lit by little mysteries.     a handful
a breath
          of what the dark
          wood took.

### hardon ('get one today'

It's a south wind that drives you back
        inside        your dream is her dream
you imagine the world as a giant flitch
curing in the cold smokehouse, of
time, were you going to say? stop while you're ahead.
                                As you
                    climb the steps
there's a smell of toast
& the sound of Elgar on the breakfast programme
comes out your neighbour's open door
the young woman stands there        her clouds of sleep
burn off        morning breezes into her dark house
she has her baby under one arm
                            you want
                    sunshine on her breasts. Instead
you go up the steps to your room to write
you have this funny idea that the world is bacon
                                        you have to
see what you can make of it. Title: *Full Moon in Gemini:
Killing the Pig*. where frost & moonlight were . . .
Remember Auntie May at Tuamarina years ago?
how the old lady ran into the sty
            to catch the blood in a milking bucket?
black puddings        white puddings        guts hung & stripped
in the barn
                    sage in the sausages        brawns
you'd find pig toenails in.
                            Opposing eye to opposing
ear        where those lines cross on the forehead your
bullet scrambles the pig's cupful
of perceptions.        Imagine! if your beautiful neighbour was a
farmer's daughter you could unbutton her warm work-shirt
                            in the barn you
                could be happy to just go on missing out
        on all the fun
'out there'

# TONY BEYER

## *Cornwallis*

the sea has held me
by the foot
since I was five
and I fear the journey
inland as a mountain
child fears strange
grey hills
that prowl and change

nose deep in froth
and kelp shards
I have watched my father
dragging a shark rent
net to the beach

*daddy what if the shark*
                    but he
just bent his bare arms
to the hauling
and spat on the real
wet enemy who harbours
assassins and thieves

my brother was four then
slept with a dead sprat
under our pillow
stinking the place out

decoy
for sharks in the night


## *The Seventies*

it is to be my last good memory of you

sitting in the shade of a wide phoenix
palm in the asylum grounds
uninterrupted by the distant *tock*
of cricket between the staff and a
visiting team
                all tanned fit men

you have some books and a shirt
still wrapped on your knee
and I roll the dreadful RSA tobacco
you claim each week as a gift
for me in spite of your disapproval
of the one bad habit we do not share

as usual our eyes speak better than
our mouths and search each other's
faces with an intemperate hunger
yours to find something of what you
once were and mine appalled
to see what I shall probably become

you are not ill or distraught or drunk
or ever to be entirely the same again
and from a porch across the lawn
ambiguously fenced for safety
a shrivelled woman in a chair shouts
threats and obscenities at no one we know

## A Comfort Stop

when summer calls
the mad women
of the district

in their rat
bitten furs
and running shoes

their mouths
aglare like wounds
migrate from

cinema porches
nodding at the
silent question

they forever
answer yes to
and horrified

by rubbish bins
and lovers
take the sun

between their knees
in recompense
for common rites

of skin their
dark sorority
exempts them from


## Cut Lilac

the dead smell the rain gives
to bunches of cut lilac
in bay windowed living rooms

is another version of the skull
your mouth feels when you kiss
a lover's or a child's clear forehead

but these are impetuous blue
upon the stems that throng
the vase's throat and splay from it

half captive or as free
as wands of light the recent sun
by peering wetly forth outside

has interspersed among them
divining paths like ours in time
that sprawl and gather haltingly

towards the next blind cervix
of the grave the best of us
will shoulder through with joy

# MURRAY EDMOND

*An Afternoon in the Garden*

for Ruth

We are a little frightened of each other,
you so little, and me so big (beside you),
so the decorum of our conversation is enormous.

Seeing a snail on the concrete steps
we choose to talk to the snail
rather than to each other.

You like talking when I am round
and I like being round when you are talking.
Now you are talking to a cardboard box

in the long grass which you call first a bus,
then a boat, and later a picnic. (I was using it
as a wheelbarrow to cart the weeds

to the rubbish heap.) And the snail
has crawled away to hide from the sun
under a plastic pudding plate.

Who are you talking to, talking and talking like that?
It is not to me, and it is not to you.
It is not even to the snail or the box or the
        wheelbarrow.

You are talking to a third person, a secret person,
who stands beside us in the garden, invisible,
and suffers to listen to everything you say.

And what you say takes the form of a prayer,
as this poem does, now, too.
A prayer for you, a poem for you, a time together.

### Telephoning It

walk down the hall
(the wind outside)
pick up the phone
and make the call
(wish it was so simple) –
had such trouble before
sending news of death
or loss
down the telephone

      wires

(shimmering in the wind)

even writing a letter,
my heart fast
and my hand slow

      the voice at the other end
catches my breath, catches my news
before it's told
      The letter goes on opening
forever on a marble table top
in a foreign post office

      You, my brother,
your careful, gentle words
rising like wind
      she is dead
I know, I know, I know


2


now let us go back together
to the first line and name her death
there, so at the end

she may rise to the surface
like a bell ringing
   in sleep,
      in sleep,
         in sleep


3


today is the day
today is the day

the first day of spring

the seventh day
of the seventy-seventh year
even though it is
the eighth month.

From now on I wait –

until the telephone rings

I wait for your news

What is the time in Canterbury?
are you still at Roper Road? or
have you gone to the hospital
already? does the sun shine?
does the wind blow? do you still
drive the old citroen? is there
rust in the doors? are you driving it
now?
     I am wheeling my mind like a wind
in the direction, I am winding out my mind
like a wire down the road you travel,
I am writing out this nativity
sitting on the dark side of the world
turning my words to face the light.

4

waiting for news that is
dipped in electricity

the falling voice
the falling wire
the falling bird

We too have news,
a secret she carries inside her now
and for two months more

it is news I touch in the night
beneath her skin
gliding, the bones gliding
all night while we lie still,
someone is swimming to the surface
of our sleep.

## Stopping the Heart

1

Buying the book at last
I've heard so much about
I read and read with eyes that
take up paragraphs at a gulp
until I realise it's pretty
ordinary stuff and slow the pace

to wonder to myself how could I
have pondered intensely my reply
to this, my stance, my attitude,
(it simply fades
how could I wonder how could I
greet it

it does not stop my heart


2


Manawatu
coming up off the plains climbing
with a loaded vision in my mind
climbing to a new town
through a line of trees
called millionaire's mile
where the romney studs stand and stare
from fat dulleyed paddocks
manawatu manawatu
something beating in my hand
like a captured frog.

I carry a vision with me
of what it will be like
but the heart stops
on arriving there

                    coming before my coming
                    the first pakeha people
                    carrying among other heavy things
                    their particular vision of it
                    'Birmingham' and a grand street plan
                    still there

spreads round me
as we cruise in
down deserted mainstreet
where I had looked for
in my prescription
flatness bareness
and instead I have these hills
this mist, mirrored windows
from abandoned shops
the creaky golden leaves

of spring growth along
the football field and
rhododendrons

and later, talking
to the kids in school
we agree it could be
better like it is than

          was meant to be

We share the gap between the vision of what was meant
to be and this reality, but truly, faithfully
this joke hides our disappointment of
how it is, lying about us,
inhabited in half a way

          but does not hide my present joy
of talking with these kids of now
and of the past, acting out their history,
building for each other
a common vision to inhabit

          the wall of rhododendrons
      which encloses the playground
      makes a secret garden,
      a living ordered place arrived in
         through a small gate
      unseen except by the coming in
      like all spaces/to be in
          to inhabit totally.

The headmaster tells me
how it was a month ago.

In full flower.

My vision races back.
I rearrive.
      Misread this
last word I write
         'dreamwise'

3

The book on the table.
The book beside me.
The book I have closed
is a closed book
because the groundplan
has never been built
never walked on and
walked round in.
What I have to say
of it is bland.

In the stead of it
rose up this rose tree
bush and branch and beating heart
completely in another time and place
another space
more real and more inconclusive
for being
totally inhabited.

## My Return to Czechoslovakia

1

This is my return to Czechoslovakia.
Twice in my life I have felt utterly
foreign, staying in a place.
The first was in Prague.
I felt the need to leave behind me
a book I had written myself
– a present for the people I stayed with.
It was as though time stopped
and I needed to rest, and in their house
I rested. At night I rested
and listened to the one cold water tap
running all night in Prague,

running on and on like silence.
By day they took me by the hand
and showed me the churches, the palace,
the cathedral with the tiny window
up high where Kafka wrote and looked down
and saw the drama of K. and the priest.
They took me in hand and led me
down that long side street by the Vlatva
to a place where on a brick
at the corner of a building
at the height of my eye
some one had scratched the name Dubcek.
Because nothing seemed to correspond
I needed to leave something complete
that would stay there,
that would live its own life there.
This is my return to Czechoslovakia.


2


The second place I left a book behind me
was Christchurch, night of a lunar eclipse,
and I sat alone in the middle of a garden
perched on a chair, a singular point
in the whole of the Canterbury Plains.
I watched the moon disappear
and thought of myself as the sum
of all the people who went into my making
– my father's stoop, my mother's hands,
grandmother's hips, my Scottish soul,
doctor, preacher, grocer, weaver,
silent, dead, mad and drowned,
and not one present beside me
to watch the moon turn black.
The tide of everything being born and dying
stopped for a time in the eclipse
and I looked right through the window of the moon
– right through into Czechoslovakia.

# CILLA McQUEEN

### Matinal

Alice on the croquet lawn
is nibbling      at the morning:
high     as a tree     she is
appropriately placed for
contemplation.
            In the garden
held down by webs
                anchored on
leaves, quiet as trickling
the wind unknots its branches.
Alice goes in      to the garden
leaf by     leaf: such small things
as transparency in the sun's light
move her.
         The blackbird directs an eye
at veins      under the
skin: she watches a moment, and
laughs her
         disappearing laugh, unpicking
nets of shadows.
          Alice's balance
is delicate:
        yet see
the quiet spider journeying
from point to point,
repairing her small wounds.


### Weekend Sonnets

i

Winter's a finger under the wool, spreading
capillaries of shivers: my boots go gong on
the pavement,

I bow to the hungry letterboxes
past Joe's goat & the ship in the bottle in the
window & the kids repairing the old car
all colours & bits & pieces & rust colours
in the corrugated iron fence & the hulls of
ships, gulls wheeling slow
                              & the inkeeper's
daughter down by the water feeding the ducks,
her long striped hair clean as flax:
                              delicate,
the way she divides the bread      And here we
are at the pub, Mungo singing Whistle wind oh
whistle window Whistle me
                              Oh a ship so tall
but he's too drunk to go fishing today


                              ii


She's feeding the water, crumbling &
crumbling her white
                              hands, her eyes
colour of water, absent
                              soft voices of
ducks around her feet:
                              he's cocked keen
as a red-eyed gull watching: if he could
just beat up high into the wind & drop her
like a crab she'd split
                              & he would feed
on the milk inside her wrists
                              Love
like a round white shell skips out
over the water where it blobs & flecks
darkly under the boats
                              making sweet
lost faces drowned in nets, mussel-shell
sky full of soft hair
                              & all of the blue-lipped
hills in their eyes.

### To Ben, at the lake

See, Ben, the water
has a strong soft skin,
and all the insects dance
and jump about on it –
for them it's safe as
springy turf. You see,
it is a matter of ensuring
that you are lighter
than the medium you
walk on: in other words,
first check your meniscus

– and also, to hell with the
trout – you can't afford
to look down, anyway.
You and I have lots of
golden sticky clay on our
gumboots – the world
is holding us up
very well, today.

# BIBLIOGRAPHY

New Zealand may be assumed to be the place of publication unless otherwise stated.

JAMES K. BAXTER
  *Beyond the Palisade*, Caxton Press, 1944.
  *Blow, Wind of Fruitfulness*, Caxton Press, 1948.
  *Poems Unpleasant* (with Anton Vogt and Louis Johnson), Pegasus Press, 1952.
  *The Fallen House*, Caxton Press, 1953.
  *The Iron Breadboard, Studies in New Zealand Writing*, Mermaid Press, 1957.
  *The Night Shift, Poems on Aspects of Love* (with Charles Doyle, Louis Johnson, and
    Kendrick Smithyman), Capricorn Press, 1957.
  *In Fires of No Return*, Oxford University Press, London, 1958.
  *Howrah Bridge and Other Poems*, Oxford University Press, London, 1961.
  *Pig Island Letters*, Oxford University Press, London, 1966.
  *The Lion Skin*, The Bibliography Room, University of Otago, 1967.
  *The Rock Woman: Selected Poems*, Oxford University Press, London, 1969.
  *Jerusalem Sonnets*, The Bibliography Room, University of Otago, 1970.
  *Autumn Testament*, Price Milburn, 1972.
  *Runes*, Oxford University Press, London, 1973.
  *The Labyrinth*, Oxford University Press, 1974.
  *Collected Poems*, Oxford University Press, 1979.

TONY BEYER
  *Jesus Hobo*, Caveman Press, 1971.
  *The Meat*, Caveman Press, 1974.
  *Dancing Bear*, Melaleuca Press, 1981.

CHARLES BRASCH
  *The Land and the People and Other Poems*, Caxton Press, 1939.
  *The Quest*, a verse play, The Compass Players, London, 1946.
  *Disputed Ground, Poems 1939–45*, Caxton Press, 1948.
  *The Estate and Other Poems*, Caxton Press, 1957.
  *Ambulando*, Caxton Press, 1964.
  *Not Far Off*, Caxton Press, 1969.
  *Home Ground*, Caxton Press, 1974.

ALISTAIR CAMPBELL
  *Mine Eyes Dazzle, Poems 1947–9*, Pegasus Press, 1950; revised editions, 1951 and
    1956.
  *Sanctuary of Spirits*, Wai-Te-Ata Press, 1963.
  *Wild Honey*, Oxford University Press, London, 1964.
  *Blue Rain*, Wai-Te-Ata Press, 1967.
  *Kapiti: Selected Poems 1947–71*, Pegasus Press, 1972.
  *Dreams, Yellow Lions*, Alister Taylor, 1975.
  *Collected Poems*, Alister Taylor, 1982.

ALLEN CURNOW

*Valley of Decision*, Phoenix Miscellany I, Auckland University College Students' Association, 1933.

*Three Poems*, Caxton Club Press, 1935.

*Enemies, Poems 1934–36*, Caxton Press, 1937.

*Not in Narrow Seas*, Caxton Press, 1939.

*Recent Poems* (with A. R. D. Fairburn, Denis Glover, and R. A. K. Mason), Caxton Press, 1941.

*Island and Time*, Caxton Press, 1941.

*Sailing or Drowning*, Progressive Publishing Society, 1943.

*Jack Without Magic*, Caxton Press, 1946.

*At Dead Low Water, and Sonnets*, Caxton Press, 1949.

*The Axe: A Verse Tragedy*, Caxton Press, 1949.

edited, *A Book of New Zealand Verse, 1923–45*, Caxton Press, 1945; revised edition, 1951.

*Poems 1949–57*, Mermaid Press, 1957.

*The Penguin Book of New Zealand Verse*, edited for Penguin Books, London, 1960.

*A Small Room with Large Windows*, Oxford University Press, London, 1962.

*Trees, Effigies, Moving Objects*, Catspaw Press, 1972.

*An Abominable Temper*, Catspaw Press, 1973.

*Collected Poems 1933–1973*, A. H. & A. W. Reed, 1974.

*An Incorrigible Music*, AUP/OUP, 1979.

*You Will Know When You Get There: Poems 1979–81*, AUP/OUP, 1982.

LAURIS EDMOND

*In Middle Air*, Pegasus Press, 1975.

*The Pear Tree*, Pegasus Press, 1977.

*Seven : poems*, Waysgoose Press, 1980.

*Wellington Letter: a sequence of poems*, Mallinson Rendel, 1980.

*Salt from the North*, Oxford University Press, 1980.

MURRAY EDMOND

*Entering the Eye*, Caveman Press, 1973.

*Patchwork: poems*, Hawk Press, 1978.

*End Wall*, Oxford University Press, 1981.

SAM HUNT

*Bracken Country*, Glenbervie Press, 1971.

*From Bottle Creek*, Alister Taylor, 1972.

*South into Winter: poems and roadsongs*, Alister Taylor, 1973.

*Time to Ride,* Alister Taylor, 1975.

*Drunkard's Garden*, Hampson Hunt, 1977.

*Collected Poems*, Penguin Books, 1980.

MICHAEL JACKSON

*Latitudes of Exile*, John McIndoe, 1976.

*Wall*, John McIndoe, 1980.

LOUIS JOHNSON

Stanza and Scene, Handcraft Press, 1945.

The Sun Among the Ruins, Pegasus Press, 1951.

Roughshod Among the Lilies, Pegasus Press, 1951.

Poems Unpleasant (with James K. Baxter and Anton Vogt), 1952.

The Dark Glass, Handcraft Press, 1955.

News of Molly Bloom, Pegasus Press, 1955.

Two Poems, Pegasus Press, 1956.

New Worlds for Old, Capricorn Press, 1957.

The Night Shift, Poems on Aspects of Love (with James K. Baxter, Charles Doyle, and Kendrick Smithyman), Capricorn Press, 1957.

New Zealand Poetry Yearbook, editor, vols. I–III, Reed, 1951–3; vols. IV–XI, Pegasus Press, 1954–62, 1964.

Bread and a Pension, Pegasus Press, 1964.

The Glassy Mountain: Selected Poems, Poetry Magazine, Wellington Teachers College, 1965.

Land Like a Lizard, Jacaranda Press, Brisbane, 1970.

Onion, Caveman Press, 1972.

Selected Poems, Mitchell College of Advanced Education, Bathurst, N.S.W., 1972.

Fires and Patterns, Jacaranda Press, Brisbane, 1975.

ALAN LONEY

The Bare Remembrance, Caveman Press, 1971.

dear Mondrian, Hawk Press, 1976.

A Steal (of the best . . .), Frontiers Press, 1978.

Shorter Poems 1963–77, AUP/OUP, 1979.

RACHEL McALPINE

Lament for Ariadne, Caveman Press, 1975.

Stay at the Dinner Party, Caveman Press, 1977.

Fancy Dress, Cicada, 1979.

House Poems, Nutshell Books, 1980.

BILL MANHIRE

The Elaboration, Square & Circle, 1972.

How to Take Off Your Clothes at the Picnic, Wai-Te-Ata Press, 1977.

Good Looks, AUP/OUP, 1982.

DAVID MITCHELL

The Orange Grove, Poets' Co-operative, 1969.

Pipe Dreams in Ponsonby, Stephen Chan, 1972; reprinted, Caveman, 1975.

VINCENT O'SULLIVAN

Our Burning Time, Prometheus Books, 1965.

Revenants, Prometheus Books, 1969.

Edited An Anthology of Twentieth Century New Zealand Poetry, Oxford University Press, London, 1970.

Bearings, Oxford University Press, 1973.

*Butcher & Co.*, Oxford University Press, 1976.
*From the Indian Funeral*, John McIndoe, 1976.
*Brother Jonathan, Brother Kafka*, Oxford University Press, 1980.
*The Butcher Papers*, Oxford University Press, 1982.

## ELIZABETH SMITHER

*Here Come the Clouds*, Alister Taylor, 1975.
*You're Very Seductive William Carlos Williams*, John McIndoe, 1978.
*The Sarah Train*, Hawk Press, 1980.
*The Legend of Marcello Mastroianni's Wife*, AUP/OUP, 1981.
*Casanova's Ankle*, Oxford University Press, 1981.

## KENDRICK SMITHYMAN

*Seven Sonnets*, Pelorus Press, 1946.
*The Blind Mountain*, Caxton Press, 1950.
*The Gay Trapeze*, Handcraft Press, 1955.
*Inheritance*, Paul's Book Arcade, 1962.
*Flying to Palmerston*, Oxford University Press for Auckland University, 1968.
*Earthquake Weather*, AUP/OUP, 1972.
*The Seal in the Dolphin Pool*, AUP/OUP, 1974.
*Dwarf with a Billiard Cue*, AUP/OUP, 1978.

## C. K. STEAD

*Whether the Will is Free, Poems 1954–62*, Paul's Book Arcade, 1964.
*Crossing the Bar*, AUP/OUP, 1972.
*Quesada, Poems: 1972–74*, The Shed, 1975.
*Walking Westward*, The Shed, 1979.

## HONE TUWHARE

*No Ordinary Sun*, Blackwood and Janet Paul, 1964.
*Come Rain Hail*, The Bibliography Room, University of Otago, 1970.
*Sapwood & Milk*, Caveman Press, 1972.
*Something Nothing*, Caveman Press, 1974.
*Making a fist of it*, Jackstraw Press, 1978.
*Selected Poems*, John McIndoe, 1980.

## IAN WEDDE

*Homage to Matisse*, Amphedesma Press, London, 1971.
*Made Over*, Stephen Chan, 1974.
*Earthly: Sonnets for Carlos*, Amphedesma Press, 1975.
*Pathway to the Sea*, Hawk Press, 1975.
*Spells for Coming Out*, AUP/OUP, 1977.
*Castaly*, AUP/OUP, 1980.

# GLOSSARY OF MAORI WORDS AND PHRASES*

Te Ariki *the Lord*
Te Atua *God*

E O; *oh*

hakea *a shrub, formerly used as a hedge-plant*
hangi *earth oven; by extension, a feast*
He porangi, he tutua *a madman, a nobody*
He Waiata mo Te Kare *a song for Te Kare*
Hemi *James*
hine *girl, young woman*
Hine-nui-te-po *Goddess of Death*
Hoani *John*

inanga *a pale translucent kind of greenstone*

kahawai *species of fish,* Arripis tutta
kai *food*
Te Kare *an object of affection*
Te Kare o Nga Wai *Te Kare of the waters*
kauri *a massive coniferous forest tree, prized for
    its timber*
kina *sea egg*
kono *woven food basket*
koro *old man, father, elder male relative*
kumara *sweet potato*

Manawatu *western coastal province in lower
    North Island; literally 'heart standing still'*
mango *shark*
manuka *small shrub or tree with aromatic leaves*
marae *tribal meeting-ground*
moko *facial tattoo*

Moriori *member of an early Polynesian people,
    now extinct*

pa *Maori village, originally fortified*
pakeha *New Zealander of European descent*
pia *beer*
pohutukawa *an evergreen coastal tree with
    bright red blossom*
punga *tree-fern*

Te Ra *the sun; by extension, God*
rata *vine or tree with bright red blossom*
raupo *bulrush*
riwai *potato*

taiaha *weapon made of wood, about 5 ft. long*
'Taku ngakau ki a koe' *I give my heart to you*
Tangaroa *god of the sea*
tangi *Maori funeral ceremony; to cry*
taniko *woven band or belt*
taniwha *mythical monster inhabiting rivers or
    the sea*
ti-kouka *commonly 'cabbage tree',* Cordyline
    australis, *with distinctive long narrow leaves
    growing in tufts*
totara *a large coniferous forest tree, prized for its
    timber*
tuatara *reptile resembling a large lizard*

Te Whaea *the Source; the Mother of God*
whare *house*
wharepuni *meeting-house*
Te Whiro *God of Darkness; death*

* Proper names without an English equivalent, and place-names are not included.

# INDEX OF TITLES AND FIRST LINES

Titles are in *italics*; first lines in roman